8 Kinds of Writing

Lessons and Practice for Writing Tests and Samples

SECOND EDITION

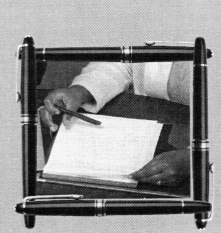

ALLEN S. GOOSE

J. WESTON

WALCH

PUBLISHER

Portland, Maine

User's Guide
to
Walch Reproducible Books

As part of our general effort to provide educational materials that are as practical and economical as possible, we have designated this publication a "reproducible book." The designation means that purchase of the book includes purchase of the right to limited reproduction of all pages on which this symbol appears:

Here is the basic Walch policy: We grant to individual purchasers of this book the right to make sufficient copies of reproducible pages for use by all students of a single teacher. This permission is limited to a single teacher and does not apply to entire schools or school systems, so institutions purchasing the book should pass the permission on to a single teacher. Copying of the book or its parts for resale is prohibited.

Any questions regarding this policy or requests to purchase further reproduction rights should be addressed to:

Permissions Editor
J. Weston Walch, Publisher
321 Valley Street • P.O. Box 658
Portland, Maine 04104-0658

1   2   3   4   5   6   7   8   9   10

ISBN 0-8251-4255-5

Copyright © 1993, 2001
J. Weston Walch, Publisher
P.O. Box 658 • Portland, Maine 04104-0658
www.walch.com

Printed in the United States of America

Contents

Chapter 4: Evaluative Writing

Chapter 5: Observational Writing

Chapter 6: Problem/Solution Writing

Chapter 7: Short Story

Chapter 8: Speculation About Causes or Effects

Appendix

To the Teacher

The 32 writings prompts in this volume have been developed over many years of classroom teaching. I have found them to be excellent tools for motivating students to write—and write well. Each prompt is designed to relate to a topic students care about—and, as we all know, when students want to write about a subject, they produce better work.

About the New Edition

This second edition of *8 Kinds of Writing* includes many new features. Each chapter has been expanded to include four writing prompts instead of the original three. Moreover, some prompts from the original edition have been replaced with new prompts; a total of 13 new prompts have been added to this edition.

Another added feature of the new edition is a graphic organizer for each chapter, tailored to the specific kind of writing being addressed. These prewriting organizers will help all students—but especially your less verbal, more visual learners—arrange their thoughts and work on important vocabulary and concepts before plunging into the first draft of any essay.

The newly added Appendix contains a correlation chart showing some of the state English/Language Arts and writing standards addressed by the various prompts in this book. The Appendix also includes some generic graphic organizers for other writing assignments, a reading group response sheet, and a page on common editing marks.

The prompts are divided into the eight writing styles tested by the California Direct Writing Test for the eighth grade. These eight styles are also included in the tests administered by most other states. These types are:

1. Autobiographical Incident
2. Information Report
3. Firsthand Biographical Sketch
4. Evaluative Writing
5. Observational Writing
6. Problem/Solution Writing
7. Short Story
8. Speculation About Causes or Effects

Each chapter begins with an overview of the writing style being addressed, one version for the teacher, and one for the student.

Holistic Grading

Although these prompts are meant to be graded holistically, grading shouldn't exclude mechanics, grammar, and spelling. Writing conventions should be included in the final evaluation of the whole work. While they may seem diametrically opposed, holistic grading and conventional grading can actually complement each other. I still use holistic methods for assessing for final grades, but I also apply conventional standards in the assessment. And, I will turn papers back to writers who have made errors in spelling, grammar, or mechanics and will demand that they be corrected. This leads to great improvement in mastery of all of the content areas. I have actually been able to link overall student success to improvements

made in grammar, spelling, and neatness. Learners find revising their work for conventions very tedious work, however. You have to keep reminding them that the reward for this tedious work is a better grade at the end.

The Prompts

Each writing prompt in this volume has three parts. The first part is the writing situation, or "stage setting." The purpose of this part is to get students into the writing. In most of the prompts, this simply involves reading a few lines; in a few cases, I have suggested some prewriting activities to help get students started.

The second part of the prompt gives the specific directions for writing. Students are told to whom they should address their writing, what should be included in their essay, and what their grade will be based on. Including this information on the prompt sheet ensures that all learners have the information they need to complete the assignment successfully.

The third part of the prompt offers several prompt notes, or hints, about ways in which students can make their writing effective. These tips will help writers focus on what is most important in each individual writing prompt.

Revision Guide (First Draft Guide)

The first draft should be written in one class period. The actual writing time should be about 45 minutes. Many students have trouble with this time limit at first. You may find that suggesting some kind of prewriting organization will help them arrange their thoughts; the graphic organizer for each chapter in this book will be of great help here. Emphasize to students that they will

have a chance to revise and improve their work. I have included a first draft/revision guide because I found that many of my best students skimped this part of the assignment. Including a grade for the first draft cured this. When students have completed their first drafts, they should hand them in. You can then return the writing and the prompt sheet with the completed revision guide.

The revision guide will help students improve their work. It includes the key characteristics that students need to emphasize in each of the eight types of writing. You can focus on these key characteristics in your suggestions to writers, or you can take another direction if you prefer. This can also be a good place to let students know what they did well in writing to the prompt. Looking for what a student does well gives that writer the incentive to do better, and it generally sets a positive tone.

Final Draft Checklist

This checklist appears just after the revision guide for each writing prompt. Students should complete this checklist before turning in their final drafts for assessment and grading. This checklist can easily be used in other course work in which students are required to write multi-paragraph essays.

Grading Rubric

This part of the writing prompt gives students the maximum response about their work. This rubric includes the most important factors required of each particular type of writing. In most cases, items listed in the revision guide are restated; other factors are also added to enhance students' writing.

Again, the most important thing to remember in grading these papers is to give students credit for what they do well. Even the worst writer does something well, and nothing discourages a student more than having work picked apart. When students who are just beginning to express themselves formally in writing get their papers back covered in red ink, they seldom want to work hard to improve. Be purposeful with your red ink. If a student's writing has many defects, concentrate on one at a time. This will lead to more improvement than if you try to correct all the defects at once. Let your students know that you appreciate their efforts. You'll find that a little praise goes a long way.

Grading Scale

This edition of *8 Kinds of Writing* takes a slightly modified approach to grading, which reflects current best practice in secondary school teaching.

Think of each number in the boxed grading scale below as meeting some degree of standard achievement along a continuum. This is a useful scale to go by.

---

1 Minimal achievement or limited understanding
Student writes just a few words that are either minimally or not at all related to the subject.

2 Some evidence of achievement
Student writes about the subject, but is not clear and doesn't cover very many aspects of the prompt.

3 Adequate achievement
Student covers all aspects of the prompt, but the paragraphs lack the extra details and effort needed to make the writing above average.

4 Commendable achievement
Parts of the student's essay are outstanding, but other parts are rather ordinary.

5 Exceptional achievement
This student's essay is outstanding in every way, showing a consistently high level of detail and effort.

Visual Organizers

Many charts and other organizers have been included to help you use the prompts in the most efficient manner. They may also help your writing lessons go more smoothly.

- A **Correlations Chart** on state English/Language arts and writing standards is included in the Appendix of this book. This will help you track key learning goals in your lesson plans; where possible, it shows how the lessons in this book are tied to the standards. The California state standards were used in compiling this chart. However, much of the wording and many of the learning objectives appear to be nearly identical from one state to the next. At the bottom of the chart in the Appendix, a web site that includes all the state standards has been listed. This is a useful site if you want to make sure you are

addressing critical state standards in your teaching.

- **Graphic Organizers** are included in several forms:

  ◆ **Prewriting graphic organizers** are specified for the type of writing, and generic to be used for all the prompts in that chapter.

  ◆ Two **generic graphic organizers** for any type of writing have been included in the Appendix. It is helpful to try to give students a choice of organizer.

    1. The "mind map" generic organizer for a five-paragraph essay is for students who are more right-brained.

    2. The outline form of the generic organizer seems to work best for students who are more left-brained.

  ◆ A **read-around organizer** has also been included in the Appendix. This is for teachers who like to have students involved in the revision process. This organizer was designed for a committee of four to do the read-around.

- A list of **common editing marks** is also found in the Appendix. These marks are slightly different from standard marks, because I find that students often have problems interpreting the standard marks. You can use these marks to communicate changes to students, and students can use them for their own revisions and for peer editing.

Good luck with your writing instruction. These creative prompts should help motivate your students and prepare them for the many situations in which their essay-writing skills may be assessed.

Name _____

Date _____

To the Student

The writing prompts in this book are designed to help you improve the way you write. The emphasis here isn't on vocabulary and spelling but on how well you get an idea across. Each prompt includes a grading rubric to tell you how well you're doing and where you need to improve your work.

These prompts focus on eight different kinds of writing:

1. Autobiographical Incident
2. Information Report
3. Firsthand Biographical Sketch
4. Evaluative Writing
5. Observational Writing
6. Problem/Solution Writing
7. Short Story
8. Speculation About Causes or Effects

As you develop your skills in each of these different styles, your overall writing ability will improve. The mechanics of your writing will be assessed, but you will be expected to concentrate on the content and overall expression of your writing.

The Prompts

The first part of each writing prompt gives the "writing situation," the background information you need to start your writing. The second part of the prompt gives specific directions for the piece of writing: whom you will be addressing as you write, what should be included in your writing, and what your teacher will be grading you on. The third part includes "prompt notes," which highlight possible problem areas and remind you of what to focus on in your writing.

Before beginning to write for each prompt, read through the Writing Situation and Directions for Writing to be sure you know what is required by the prompt. Is a specific writing format called for? Whom are you addressing in your writing? You should also look at the Prompt Notes. You may also want to review the items in the Revision Guide and Grading Rubric, which your teacher will use to grade your writing. If you make sure you cover each of these areas as you write, you can be sure of doing well.

The First Draft

Your first draft should take you about 45 minutes to write. At first, you may find it hard to organize your thoughts and get them down in writing within this time limit, but it will get easier with practice. Using a graphic organizer—either one you create, or one your teacher gives you—can help you organize your ideas.

Remember: Although it is graded, this is only a first draft. You will have the opportunity to revise and improve your work. In grading this first draft, your teacher will be making sure that you are following the directions given in the prompt and that you have gotten off to a good start with your writing. Your teacher will use the Revision Guide to point out any areas that need improvement.

When you have finished your first draft, hand it in. It will be graded according to the Revision Guide.

(continued)

To the Student (continued)

Final Draft

Use your teacher's comments to help you revise your first draft into a final draft. When you have finished revising your first draft, attach it to your final draft. Then hand in all your work.

Your teacher will grade you on how well you followed the directions given in the prompt and how well you have expressed your ideas. The specific factors being considered are included in the Grading Rubric; you can use the Rubric as a guide while you write, to make sure you communicate your ideas clearly to your reader.

Your ability to use proper English and good spelling affects the way people see your work. Although your first duty as a writer is to write stories that stimulate and excite their readers, you must also present the reader with a legible manuscript using good mechanics.

Here is a short checklist to use in preparing your final draft:

Final Draft Checklist

_____ 1. Did you check all spelling?

_____ 2. Did you check for proper punctuation?

_____ 3. Did you check for capitalization?

_____ 4. Did you turn in a paper that is neat and clean?

_____ 5. Did you write to the proper audience?

_____ 6. Did you answer the prompt demands?

_____ 7. Did you write at least five paragraphs?

_____ 8. Did you put the proper heading on your paper?

_____ 9. Did you put your name on the paper?

_____ 10. Did you do your best work?

Chapter 1 | Autobiographical Incident

Chapter 1: Autobiographical Incident

The autobiographical incident is the easiest writing style for middle school students. They are able to write about their adventures with ease. They find that they can write about their own experiences and have people accept them as valid subjects for essays. Because of this, the autobiographical incident is often the first style in which students write successfully. This success is usually enough to get the student to go on to other writing forms.

Autobiographical incident is a personal story—of either triumph or disaster—told by a person to whom it happened. This incident takes place within a limited time. Thus, when writing about a baseball game that had special significance in the writer's life, the writer should focus only on the critical part of the game.

This writing style demands that the writer engage the reader from the beginning. Students should be taught the importance of an outstanding introduction. You may want to read stories with great beginnings to give your students models, and to show them how to adapt another author's style to their own.

One way to get students started is by showing them how television programs and commercials engage their viewers. On a videotape, string together several commercials and teasers of television shows popular with students. Another approach is to read the opening paragraphs of a few of your own favorite books. A third way to get this idea across is to use some unique way to begin your class, several days in a row. This helps students see that you can devise an unusual beginning for almost anything.

A successful piece of autobiographical incident writing demands a well-told story and rich sensory details. This is a good style for getting students to expand their sensory vocabulary. Compile a list of words students might use to relate sensory details to the reader, e.g., vast, smooth, buzz, fresh, bitter. Emphasize the fact that this method helps to engage the reader. Students quickly become motivated as they see people enjoying their work.

A final characteristic of this type of writing is self-disclosure on the writer's part—that is, displaying something the writer has learned or felt as a result of the incident. Many students find this very difficult. It is hard for them to verbalize their feelings in a way that adults find acceptable. Point this out to your students, and guide them in developing this aspect of their writing.

Graphic Organizer

The prewriting organizer for the autobiographical incident focuses on the most important characteristics of this kind of writing. Students are asked to choose a single incident in their lives about which to write; this organizer will help them stick to just that one incident. They are also required to list all the sensory words they will be using in their essays. Finally, they are prompted to think about and summarize the personal learning they have gained from the incident they describe. This type of self-analysis is a difficult skill for many students to master. They should be encouraged to include this personal learning in the conclusions of their essays.

Autobiographical Incident
Prompt Notes

Murphy's Law

- This essay is a good way to emphasize humor in students' writing.

- Talk about the importance of the first paragraph in writing.

- Work on conclusions.

- You might want either to assign or to read some humorous short stories to your class. Many of James Thurber's short stories work well as models for this prompt.

So I Panicked

- Share a panic story of your own.

- Have students share their ideas out loud.

- List words that show panic on the board.

- Remind students about the importance of using details.

- Remind students to use words that evoke excitement.

The Old Man

- Prewriting: Read Edgar Allan Poe's "The Tell-Tale Heart."

- Point out that the whole story took place in a matter of days.

- Discuss the use of flashbacks in writing.

- The significance of the encounter is important. You may need to explain what the significance of an encounter is. This might be accomplished by telling personal stories about significant people in your life.

An Odd Occurrence on Hollingworth Street

- Hollingworth Street runs directly in front of this author's school. The name is intended to be used symbolically.

- Remind students that this event can be either real or imaginary. In both cases, however, they need to remember to include vivid descriptions relating to all five senses.

- Since their peers will be able to relate to each student essay, writers need to make this event dramatic enough to capture and keep their audience's attention.

- Remind students to write about the personal learning they gained from this incident.

Name _____

Date _____

Five-Paragraph Essay:
Autobiographical Incident

Directions: Write a few words that describe a single event or incident in the box marked "A single event." In the diamond below the box, note the audience this piece is being written for. In the octagon below, write sensory words that you will use in your paragraphs. Then think about the things you learned because of this event or incident. Make note of them in the bottom box in the right column. In the five ovals on the left, note what you will say in each paragraph. Now use these notes to build your paragraphs for this essay.

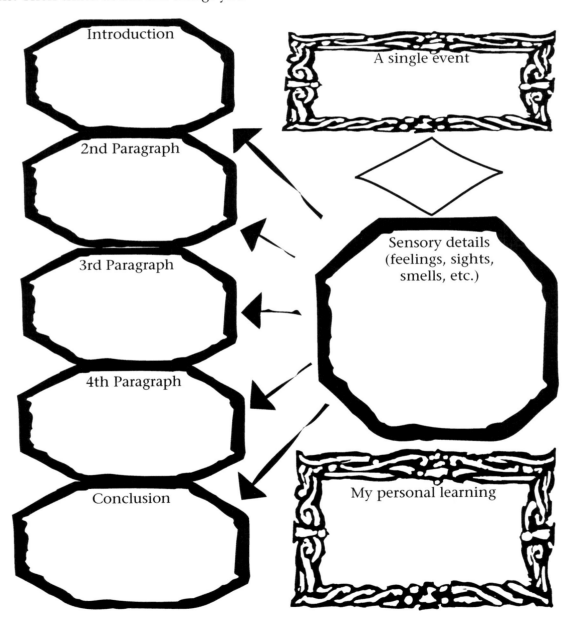

© 1993, 2001 J. Weston Walch, Publisher

5

8 Kinds of Writing

REVISION GUIDE AND GRADING RUBRIC

Name _____

Date _____

Autobiographical Incident

Title: Murphy's Law _____
So I Panicked _____
The Old Man _____
An Odd Occurrence on Hollingworth Street _____

Revision Guide	Y/N
You start this paper in a way that makes me want to keep reading.	
Suggestions: _____ _____ _____ _____	
You include your feelings, and the lessons you learned. You have included vivid details of the events you describe.	
Suggestions: _____ _____ _____ _____	

Final Draft Checklist

Check the essay's needs:

Spelling check   _____
Grammar check   _____
Verb usage   _____
Paragraphs   _____
Organization   _____
Single incident   _____
Great showing   _____

Grading Rubric

1 = minimal   5 = exceptional

1. You have produced a narrative that is dramatically written. You used more than one strategy to tell your incident.

   1   2   3   4   5

2. You wrote this for the stated audience. You present the scene, context, and people involved in this incident in a vivid manner.

   1   2   3   4   5

3. You explain the importance of this incident. You tell about any lessons that you learned.

   1   2   3   4   5

4. You have an engaging introduction and conclusion. Your writing contains at least five paragraphs. You use good spelling and grammar. The neatness of the paper shows great care.

   1   2   3   4   5

First Draft Grade	**FINAL GRADE**

STUDENT INFORMATION SHEET

Name _____

Date _____

Chapter 1
Autobiographical Incident

An **autobiographical incident** is a personal story told by the person it happened to. When you write an autobiographical incident, you are writing about yourself, your own life and experiences.

A typical feature of this type of writing is that it **takes place over a limited time**. Thus, if you are writing about a baseball game that had particular significance in your life, you only need to focus on the critical part of the game. If your great realization, humiliation, or triumph came in the third inning, you don't need to give a detailed account of the whole game. Concentrate on the important period.

One of the most important things about this type of writing is **beginning your piece** well. Why should people want to read about your life? If the opening sentence of your piece is strong enough, readers will want to know more. Look at the way other authors begin their stories to learn how to capture a reader's interest right from the start.

To be successful, autobiographical incident writing demands a **well-told story** and **rich sensory details**. Try to use words that convey information to the senses—how a thing looks, feels, sounds, smells, tastes. Use of these words helps to engage the reader.

A final characteristic of this type of writing is **self-disclosure**—revealing something that you felt or learned as a result of the incident. You may find it hard, especially at first, to put your feelings into words. Don't be discouraged by the difficulty. Keep trying. Not only will your writing improve, you may also find yourself understanding your own feelings better!

Graphic Organizer

The prewriting organizer for the autobiographical incident will help you focus on the most important characteristics of this kind of writing. You will be asked to name a *single event/incident*. You will need to include all the sensory words you are going to use in your essay. Finally, in the bottom right corner of the organizer, you will be asked to write what personal learning experience you gained from this incident. Try to use this statement in your essay's conclusion.

Chapter 1:
Autobiographical Incident

Murphy's Law

Writing Situation

You wake up, and the clothes you wanted to wear are in the laundry. Your parent yells at you for not doing something. You miss the school bus. We've all had days like that, days when everything goes wrong. They seem to be covered by Murphy's Law—the law that says, "Whatever can go wrong, will go wrong."

Directions for Writing

This essay will be for your English teacher. You are to write about a day when everything bad that could happen—did. You'll want to find a unique way of beginning your essay. Include all the emotions you felt that day, as well as vivid details about everything that happened. You'll also want to write about any lessons you learned. Your conclusion should pull all the parts of the paper together.

Prompt Notes

- A humorous approach can work well in this essay.
- Remember the importance of the first paragraph in writing.
- Work on a good conclusion.

Chapter 1:
Autobiographical Incident

So I Panicked

Writing Situation

You're walking down a street when something startles you. You're riding your bicycle when suddenly a small animal runs in front of you. You panic, not wanting to hurt the animal. You're washing your parents' party dishes. The main serving dish—the family heirloom—slips out of your hands. It heads for the tile floor, ready to shatter into a thousand pieces. You panic!

Directions for Writing

Write an article for the school literary magazine. Write about a time when you were doing something and the unexpected happened. Your readers will want to know every detail of the event and how you felt about it. You should make this article five paragraphs long. It should have a great beginning and a strong conclusion. Make sure you use your best punctuation and grammar. Poor spelling will take away from the overall effectiveness of your essay.

Prompt Notes

- Brainstorm to think of words that show panic.
- Remember the importance of using details to describe something clearly, like your feelings of panic.
- Be sure to use words that show excitement.

Chapter 1:
Autobiographical Incident

The Old Man

Writing Situation

"I once ran into an old man. His face still haunts me. I often use his face when I describe an old man." These are the opening lines of a story based on a true incident. We often run into people who haunt our lives. Sometimes they add meaning to our lives. Sometimes they provide stories to tell our friends and relatives. Sometimes they become a reference point in our lives.

Directions for Writing

Write an essay for your art teacher about meeting an old man. Your teacher will want to know, in detail, all the man's physical features. Your teacher will want to know how the old man moves, what activities he engages in, and what he had to say to you. Your teacher will also be interested in the setting and context of this meeting. Last, your teacher will want to know the importance of this meeting.

Prompt Notes

- Prewriting: Read Edgar Allan Poe's "The Tell-Tale Heart." Notice that the whole story took place in a matter of days.
- Consider using flashbacks in your writing.
- Be sure to tell readers the significance of this encounter.

Chapter 1:
Autobiographical Incident

An Odd Occurrence on Hollingworth Street

Writing Situation

You are walking down Hollingworth Street, the street that runs directly in front of your school. Right there in front of your eyes you see the strangest thing that you've ever seen in your life. You wonder if you are really seeing this happen, or if it's just a figment of your imagination.

Directions for Writing

Write an essay for your school's literary magazine. In it, describe a real or imagined incident that took place on "Hollingworth Street," either going to or from school. Your readers will want to know all the details of the incident and how you took part in it. Your readers will want you to recount this scene with great sensory detail. (Use sight, touch, smell, and hearing in your description.) Finally, explain how this incident affected your life.

Prompt Notes

- Assume that Hollingworth Street is the street that runs directly in front of your school.
- This can be either an imaginary or a real event.
- Make this event very exciting, since your classmates will relate to the area you are describing.
- Don't forget to tell about what you learned through this experience.

Chapter 2 | Information Report

Chapter 2: Information Report

If a student is able to gather facts, organize them, and use them to relate some learning to another person through writing, that student is able to write an information report. Students can use all kinds of resources, such as periodicals, newspapers, encyclopedias, the Internet, and television, to gather information. They can also call on their own experience and knowledge. They are then asked to disseminate this information to the reader.

Completing this task calls for both higher- and lower-level thinking skills. Students are called upon to recall facts, list details, and cite examples for a given subject. Accomplishing this task requires students to conceptualize, synthesize, and evaluate the information they are reporting. Students should then pull their essays together to produce conclusions that fit their theses.

The most common problem students encounter in this type of writing is organizing their material. They do well at gathering the information but find it hard to shape the material into a good essay. Exercises in organizing writing can help here. I often use a three-stage process. First, I have students gather their information. Next, I teach them clustering and outlining, and have them apply these techniques to their work. Last, they write their essays using their outlines or clusters, crossing off the pieces they use as they finish with them.

This style lends itself to use of the Internet. There are millions of pieces of information on the Web and this style will allow the students to use it to their advantage. The major problem with using the Internet is plagiarism. A good method for reducing Internet plagiarism is to require a printout of the web site. This will at least notify the student that you are aware of the problem.

Graphic Organizer

In this prewriting organizer, students are asked to include everything they have to say about the information presented in the first paragraph. They are then asked to judge the importance of the information and to present it in the order of importance. This will help them write the essay in a logical manner. The facts should flow to a logical conclusion.

15

Information Report
Prompt Notes

The Address

- This exercise should be given to eighth grade students toward the end of the school year.

- Explain what a commencement address is.

- Students should realize the honor of delivering this speech.

- If possible, show students an example of this kind of speech.

The Expert

- Students find this prompt challenging, as it requires them to put into words something they usually don't need to think about. Many students need to go home and play a game to answer this prompt.

- If students don't play video games, they can use any board game.

- Students often need coaching to develop a good beginning.

How to Clean a Messy Room

- Most students will have experience with this in real life, so it is easy for them to write on this subject.

- Talk to students about figurative writing.

- Discuss how to write with authority: Write as if what you are saying is true. Don't be wishy-washy.

- Discuss the different parts of writing— how to organize your writing.

- Read some good beginnings to students.

In the Chat Room

- Some students may never have experienced a chat room visit. If so, they will undoubtedly know classmates who visit chat rooms and can share some of their experiences with this form of electronic communication.

- Be sure to hold a class discussion about chat room safety; review with students any computer-usage rules established by your school and school district.

- Encourage students to discuss chat room usage with their parents and to solicit parents' opinions on this subject. Opinions may vary widely.

- Remind students that this essay is primarily focused on safety, and that this is what they need to focus on in their writing.

Name _____

Date _____

Five-Paragraph Essay: Report of Information

Directions: Reports of information should be well organized. This graphic organizer will help you organize your essay. It will also help you think about all the information you want to present in your essay, and how you might want to arrange that information. Think about how you want to introduce the subject. Then think about all the things you want to say. Write your notes in the proper spaces below.

Part One An introduction to the subject	Tell about what you are about to say.
Part Two The most important ideas from this information	Write notes that might go into the second paragraph here.
Part Three Important ideas about your subject	Write notes that might go into the third paragraph here.
Part Four Ideas that will lead to a greater understanding of the subject	Write notes that might go into the fourth paragraph here.
Part Five An ending to the subject	Give a review and a "so what" to make up your conclusion.

Name _____

Date _____

Information Report

Title:	The Address _____
	The Expert _____
	How to Clean a Messy Room _____
	In the Chat Room _____

Revision Guide	Y/N	_Grading Rubric_
You start this in a way that makes me want to continue reading. You develop a central idea.		1 = minimal 5 = exceptional 1. You present a great deal of information about your subject. The information is focused and well organized. It proceeds logically throughout your writing. **1 2 3 4 5**
Suggestions: _____ _____ _____		2. You use many different strategies in presenting your information, which makes the essay interesting. You show that you are excited about this subject. You also display authority about this subject. **1 2 3 4 5**
Your ideas are elaborated properly. You use supporting explanations. You use evidence and details effectively. These add to the strength of your essay.		3. You reveal your sources of information in a way that shows the expertise you have gained in your chosen subject. **1 2 3 4 5**
Suggestions: _____ _____ _____		4. You have a strong introduction and conclusion. Your writing contains at least five paragraphs. You use good spelling and grammar. The neatness of your paper shows great care. **1 2 3 4 5**

Final Draft Checklist

Check the essay's needs:

Spelling check _____

Grammar check _____

Verb usage _____

Paragraphs _____

Organization _____

Facts used _____

Conclusion supported _____

First Draft Grade	**FINAL GRADE**

8 Kinds of Writing

Chapter 2
Information Report

If you are able to gather facts, organize them, and use them to convey information—in writing—to another person, you are able to write an information report. Reports of this kind don't need to be confined just to information you already know. You can also use all kinds of resources—like periodicals, newspapers, encyclopedias, the Internet, and television—to gather information. Then you just need to get this information across to your readers. To do this successfully, you need to recall facts, list details, and give examples for a given subject. This means you have to evaluate your information, bring it all together, and express it in your own words.

Many students find that organizing the material is the most difficult aspect of this type of writing. They do well at gathering the information but find it hard to shape the material into an essay. If this is a problem for you, experiment with different approaches to organizing your material. Once you have gathered the information, try using it to write an outline for your essay. Or you might want to see if your information can be sorted into related groups or "clusters" of ideas. Then, as you write your essay, cross off the clusters as you finish with them. Your teacher will help you find an approach to organizing information that will work for you.

Graphic Organizer

The prewriting organizer for an informational report is similar to the kind of organizer you would use for writing a newspaper article. In the introduction, include clear information about your purpose for writing. Follow this up with everything you know of importance about the subject. Next, you need to assess what it all means—how does your essay lead to a greater understanding of the subject? Try to present your ideas in order of importance. This will help you write your essay in the most logical manner.

Name _____

Date _____

Chapter 2:
Information Report

The Address

Writing Situation

For the last two years, you have been one of the leaders in your school. Now, your fellow students have voted to have you deliver the commencement address at this year's graduation ceremony.

Directions for Writing

Write a speech explaining why your time at this school was special. Tell your listeners what you've learned at this school. Explain what makes this school special. Talk about the special relationships you have formed with your peers and teachers. Describe the kind of education you received at this school. Remember that both adults and students will be listening, and your speech should interest all of them.

Prompt Notes

- Be sure you understand what a commencement address is.
- Your speech should show that you realize the honor of delivering this speech.
- Try not to offend the adults in your audience, while not boring your fellow students.

Chapter 2:
Information Report

The Expert

Writing Situation

We all have a skill that qualifies us as an expert. Your skill might be playing a video game or a musical instrument, or repairing things, or one of dozens of other skills. Whatever it is, when people want to know about this, they come to you.

Directions for Writing

Write video game directions to go in a newsletter for people who play that particular game. Your article will need to include the scenario of the game. It must give directions that will allow the reader to win the game. You should also explain why this is a good game to play.

Prompt Notes

- Don't be surprised if you need to go home and play a video game before you can complete this report. It can be hard to put into words a process you usually do automatically.
- If you don't play video games, you can use a board game instead.
- Pay special attention to how you begin your writing.

Chapter 2:
Information Report

How to Clean a Messy Room

Writing Situation

As a teenager, your idea of what your room should look like is often different from your parents' idea of what is acceptable. This has been the cause of many arguments between teens and parents. Parents seem to want you to meet their standards of orderliness. Because of their superior position, your parents usually win out, and you have to go along with their version of a clean room.

Directions for Writing

Write an essay for your home economics teacher explaining the process you go through when your parents insist that you tidy your room. You should also describe the process your parents go through to get you to clean your room. Your teacher will want to know the state of your room before you started, and the way you go about straightening this room. Last, your teacher will want to know your feelings about doing this job before, during, and after completion. Begin your paper in a way that will capture the interest of your reader, and end in a satisfying manner.

Prompt Notes

- Organize your writing to make the whole process clear to your readers.
- Make your opening a real attention-getter.
- Write with authority; try not to be hesitant when you make a statement.

Name _____

Date _____

Chapter 2:
Information Report

In the Chat Room

Writing Situation

Today we can meet people in a way no other generation has experienced: through chat rooms on the Internet. The Internet is home to many different kinds of chat rooms. You can meet people from all over the world who have like interests. These real-time chats offer us opportunity for both mind expansion and danger. It's important that we are aware of both the courtesies and the protections we need to use these rooms to our advantage.

Directions for Writing

Write an essay for the school's parent newsletter. In it, explain to parents the benefits and dangers of letting their children use chat rooms on the Internet. You might also explain how chat rooms can be used to benefit learning. Include directions for parents' safe supervision of their children while in these rooms. You will also want to explain how to conduct yourself in one of these rooms. Your essay should be at least five paragraphs. You should use your best grammar and spelling, and turn in your neatest work.

Prompt Notes

- If you have never been in a chat room, you probably know classmates who have chat room experience.
- Ask your friends if they know anything about chat room safety and compare the answers.
- You may want to ask your parents for their opinions on the subject.
- Remember that this is a safety essay. Focus on how to make things safer.

Chapter 3 | Firsthand Biographical Sketch

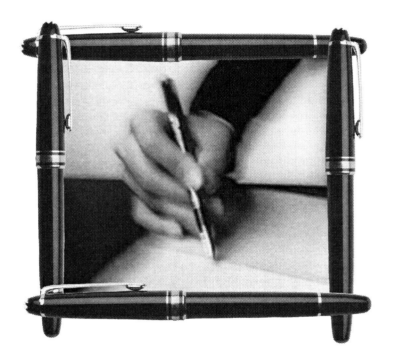

Chapter 3:
Firsthand Biographical Sketch

The reader can see the person as if he or she were standing there. This is what the writer should achieve. Students need to use words to paint a picture of the person they are writing about. They need to include all the aspects of the individual that serve to make this person unique.

Details are important. The person's appearance must be described, down to the finest points. Students must be made aware of those fine details that they see but often don't consciously register. Students are used to having visualizations constructed for them. I often find that students need to work on this skill, and I have devised several activities to help them acquire it. One favorite activity is called "guess the right picture." In this activity, several similar pictures are hung in the classroom. Students are asked to "write a painting" about one of the pictures—that is, to describe the picture in detail. The descriptions are then read aloud, so that students can compare them with the pictures. I assign points based on how many of a student's classmates can guess which picture was being described.

Another useful activity involves the reverse of this process. I read aloud a description of a creature, and students are asked to draw the creature. Points are awarded to drawings that include the details in the description. (Science fiction books and short stories are useful sources for descriptions.) Transforming words into images often makes it easier for students than to express images in words.

To succeed at this kind of writing, students must look at all aspects of the subject's personality. They need to show the actions, ideas, and feelings of their subjects. To do this, students need to use concrete examples, dialogue, and comparisons/ contrasts with other people. Students might include a triumph in the subject's life which the writer admires. However, this is usually only successful when the writer knows the subject well. I have seen a few students try to write in this way about an athlete or other "personality," but they usually don't do a particularly good job.

This type of writing calls for an expression of the writer's feelings. It doesn't matter much whether the emotion is love, hate, or admiration; it only matters that the tone of the essay is consistent. Students may develop several strategies to convey these feelings, and you should encourage experimentation. One caution: This style of writing cannot be in the first person. Many students put too many *I*'s in their writing. Remind students that they are writing about another person, and don't let them put in too many first-person pronouns. Watch for this on the first draft.

Graphic Organizer

This prewriting organizer is divided into two parts. The first part is designed to get the students thinking about the emotions and feelings that another person might have. Students need to think deeply about these emotions and how they are manifested in the person they are writing about. Use brainstorming activities to help students come up with these thoughts; for example, name an emotion, then ask how different students in the class show these emotions.

The second part of the organizer asks students to use the notes they took for the first part to organize their thoughts into paragraphs.

Firsthand Biographical Sketch
Prompt Notes

The Giving Tree

- Read Shel Silverstein's *The Giving Tree*.

- Try to steer discussion toward the tree as a representation of someone or something special.

- Work on getting students to name characteristics of someone they know who is a giver.

- Students should describe this person in detail.

- This is a good chance to use action verbs and adverbs that give deeper meanings to actions.

- Students should also use comparison in their descriptions.

Most Unusual

- Students should focus on the person's physical appearance.

- The reader should clearly understand why this person is unusual.

- The reader should be aware of the subject's effect on the writer and on others.

- This is another place to emphasize engaging the reader. You might want to read a few fine story openings to the class.

The Pencil Man

- Students should be led to describe this person fully.

- Guide students to work on the beggar's actions.

- Watch to be sure students relate the poem to their sketch.

- Dialogue can be used effectively in this sketch.

- Suggest other techniques such as flashbacks and foreshadowing.

I Am an Animal

- Be sure that students are familiar with the story of Circe from Greek mythology. Circe was a beautiful witch who was exiled to a remote island in the Aegean Sea. Odysseus and his crew had the misfortune to land on this island on their way home from the Trojan War. Circe transformed most of the men into animals; Odysseus had to use great cunning to get her to turn them back into men.

- Encourage students to consider not just the physical characteristics of various animals, but also their behavioral characteristics and "personalities."

- Emphasize the importance of creating a powerful introductory paragraph to captivate the writer's audience from the very start.

- Before students hand in their work, remind them to check to make sure they have included both physical and emotional descriptions in their writing.

Name _____

Date _____

Five-Paragraph Essay:
Firsthand Biographical Sketch

Directions: Choose the person you will write a biographical sketch about. Write all you know about that person. Then use that knowledge to plan your paragraph in the boxes that are marked for the paragraphs. In the box titled "Other things about the person," write key words that describe how knowing this person affected you. Keep this statement in mind while you are writing your essay.

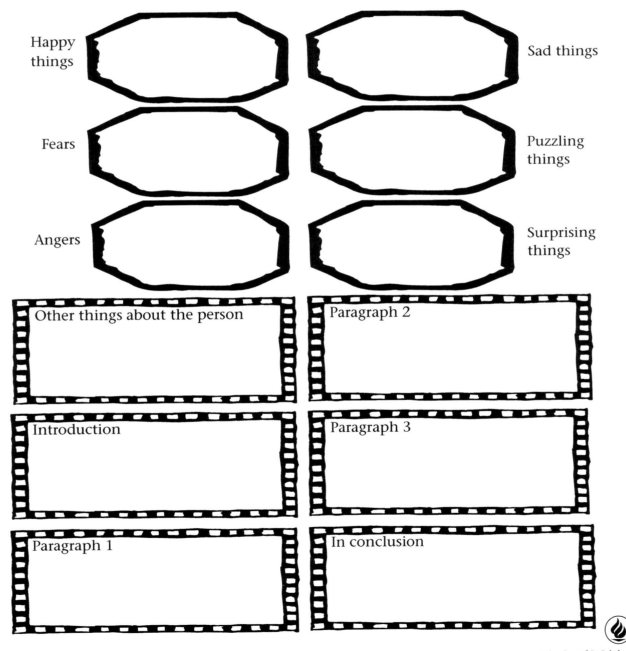

Happy things

Sad things

Fears

Puzzling things

Angers

Surprising things

Other things about the person

Paragraph 2

Introduction

Paragraph 3

Paragraph 1

In conclusion

Firsthand Biographical Sketch

Title:
The Giving Tree _____
Most Unusual _____
The Pencil Man _____
I Am an Animal _____

Revision Guide	Y/N
You present a vivid description of the person you write about. You include both actions and physical descriptions.	
Suggestions: _____ _____ _____	
You include the activities that this person engages in. You are dramatic in your descriptions. You use dialogue to explain this person's thoughts.	
Suggestions: _____ _____ _____	

Final Draft Checklist

Check the essay's needs:

Spelling check _____
Grammar check _____
Verb usage _____
Paragraphs _____
Organization _____
Told in the second person _____
"Showing" writing _____

Grading Rubric

1 = minimal   5 = exceptional

1. You present a full, vivid characterization of this person. You make this person come alive with your writing.

   1   2   3   4   5

2. You develop a good story through concrete examples and dramatic incidents. You also explain recurring activities.

   1   2   3   4   5

3. Your statement of the significance of this person in your life makes me understand why you write about him/her.

   1   2   3   4   5

4. You have a strong introduction and conclusion. Your writing contains at least five paragraphs. You use good spelling and grammar. The neatness of the paper shows great care.

   1   2   3   4   5

First Draft Grade	**FINAL GRADE**

Chapter 3
Firsthand Biographical Sketch

When your reader can see the person you are writing about as if he or she were standing there, you know you have written a successful biographical sketch. You need to use words to paint a picture of your subject. Include all the aspects of the individual that serve to make him or her unique.

Details are important. You must describe the person's appearance, down to the finest points. Sometimes we see the details but don't really register them. You may need to work on noticing details and putting them into words.

To succeed at this kind of writing, you need to look at all aspects of the subject's personality. You need to show the person's actions, ideas, and feelings. Use concrete examples, dialogue, and comparisons to make the individual stand out. You might include some triumph in your subject's life. But be careful: this usually doesn't work unless you know your subject very well. It may be tempting to write about an athlete or other "personality," but these sketches rarely succeed.

In this type of writing, you need to express your feelings. It doesn't matter whether the emotion is love, hate, or admiration; it only matters that the tone of the essay is consistent. Experiment with different ways to convey these feelings. You should be able to find a few different approaches that work for you.

Just one note of caution: Don't try to write these pieces in the first person, using *I*. You are writing about someone else, not yourself. Stick to the third person as much as possible.

Graphic Organizer

The prewriting organizer for a firsthand biographical sketch is divided into two main parts. The first part asks you to think about the emotions (the feelings) that someone else might have. You will need to think hard in some cases. Try to imagine how the person's actions and appearance would show each emotion that he or she is feeling. You may want to discuss with your classmates how they act and look when they are feeling certain ways.

The second part of the graphic organizer helps you turn your notes from the first part of the activity into logical paragraphs for your essay.

Chapter 3:
Firsthand Biographical Sketch

The Giving Tree

Writing Situation

You have read Shel Silverstein's *The Giving Tree,* and you have discussed the symbolism of this book. At times, we've all felt like that tree, giving and giving and getting nothing back in return. You may know someone who always seems to give. This person might be a parent, a teacher, or a member of the clergy. It could be a friend. In any case, this is the person you go to in a time of trouble.

Directions for Writing

Write an essay for your English teacher in which you praise the virtues of a person with the characteristics of a giving tree. Let your reader know what this person looks like, where and when you meet or talk to this person, what type of advice this person gives you, and what this person does that is important. You should describe the feelings this person evokes. Your teacher will want to know the importance of this person in your life.

Prompt Notes

- Prewriting: Read Shel Silverstein's *The Giving Tree.*
- Think of the tree as a representation of someone or something special.
- List the characteristics of people you know who are givers.
- Describe the person you choose in detail.
- Use action verbs and adverbs that give deeper meanings to actions.
- Use comparison in your descriptions.

Name _____

Date _____

Chapter 3:
Firsthand Biographical Sketch

Most Unusual

Writing Situation

We sometimes notice people who are different from everyone else. They may be different because of their jobs, looks, hobbies, behavior, and so forth. We often find that we remember these people very clearly. *Reader's Digest* used to pay $50 for stories about such unique people.

Directions for Writing

Write a story for *Reader's Digest* about an unusual person you have met. The editor of the *Digest* will want to know the person's physical characteristics and behavior. He or she will be especially interested in what makes this person unique. You will also want to describe your personal connection with this person.

Prompt Notes

- You should focus on the person's physical appearance.
- The reader should clearly understand why this person is unusual.
- The reader should be aware of the subject's effect on you and on others.
- Remember the importance of engaging the reader from the beginning.

Name _____

Date _____

Chapter 3:
Firsthand Biographical Sketch

The Pencil Man

Writing Situation

The Pencil Man
on the corner I saw him sitting
pencils and a cup
A few coins he was getting
He was blindly petting his little pup
He said don't be upset by my situation
Things are pretty good from where I be
I see more in my imagination
A world you'll never see.

Directions for Writing

This poem was written about a blind beggar. You are a tourist walking through a large city. You have met the blind beggar of this poem and talked to him for some time. He has told you how he sees the world. Back in your hotel room, write a letter to your best friend back home. In it, describe what you learned from the beggar. Your friend will want to know about the beggar's appearance, how he sounded, the conditions under which he lived. Your friend will also be interested in hearing what the beggar told you about how he saw the world. In your conclusion, tell your friend how this encounter affected you.

Prompt Notes

- You should describe this person fully.
- Work on the beggar's actions.
- Work on the relation of the poem to the biographical sketch. You can use dialogue effectively in this sketch.
- Consider other techniques, such as flashbacks and foreshadowing.

Name _____

Date _____

Chapter 3:
Firsthand Biographical Sketch

I Am an Animal

Writing Situation

In the ancient Greek epic *The Odyssey*, Odysseus's men are turned into animals by the witch Circe. We often describe people in terms of animal behavior—he moves like a panther, she's as swift as a hawk. Imagine that one day, you say the wrong thing to somebody and poof, like Odysseus's men, he or she is turned into an animal. It could be a horse, a dog, a pig—but it will be something that the person already had within.

Directions for Writing

Write an essay for the school's literary journal. In it, describe a dream that you had in which your best friend turned into an animal. In this essay, describe all the sights and sounds and smells and adventures your friend found while he/she was this animal. The feelings expressed as this animal will be important to explore. Write with your best grammar and spelling. Your essay should be at least five paragraphs long, with the first paragraph an introduction and the last paragraph a conclusion.

Prompt Notes

- Circe was a beautiful witch who was exiled to an island by the gods of ancient Greece. Odysseus and his men landed on her island on the way back to Greece. Circe turned most of the men into animals; Odysseus had to get her to turn them back to humans.
- Think about the characteristics of animals, not only physically, but also behaviorally.
- To make this essay exciting, really work on the introductory paragraph.
- Don't forget to include physical and emotional characteristics.

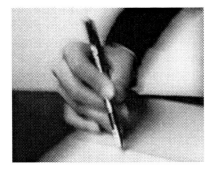

Chapter 4

Evaluative Writing

Chapter 4: Evaluative Writing

Middle school students have thousands of opinions. Ask them about any subject, and they always have something to say. Since evaluative writing asks students to give their opinions, you might think that the style and the age would be a match made in heaven. Wrong! It just doesn't translate that way. When students are asked to write an evaluation, their thinking often becomes muddled.

Evaluation as a writing style requires the student to make a judgment and state it clearly. Anything less is unacceptable in this writing style. The writer must state the strengths or weaknesses of the subject. We are often called on to make this kind of judgment in life; we often see this kind of writing in book and movie reviews. Here, the writer must use the critical thinking skills of analysis, synthesis, and evaluation.

Once the judgment is made, the writer must persuade the reader of the correctness of the arguments in order to prove the validity of the point. Comparisons and contrasts, examples, anecdote, and description are among the strategies the writer might use to do this. The writer's opinion must be supported by clearly developed proofs.

Organization is valuable here, and should not be overlooked. You cannot overemphasize the fact that the student's task is to give logical arguments that support the main conclusion. Many students are able to make the original judgment required for this writing type, but fall down on backing the judgment up with argument. These arguments should borrow from the characteristics of both the Information Report and Observational Writing. The arguments included in the essay should lead to a natural conclusion.

Finally, the student must set a tone that is appropriate for the subject under consideration. This tone should be set in the opening paragraph and followed through to the end of the essay.

Graphic Organizer

This prewriting organizer starts with the central question of the judgment. This is the hardest part for students of this age to state clearly. The organizer then guides students through the different reasons that have led students to their judgment. All three of these reasons should support the conclusion.

Evaluative Writing
Prompt Notes

My Auto

- The challenge here for students is going beyond the looks of the car.

- In prewriting exercises, get students to talk about other valuable aspects of automobiles, such as:
  reliability
  psychological effect

- Get a car magazine and read about an automotive test drive.

- Make sure that students' essay form follows the newspaper article structure.

The Starry Night

- Collect copies of van Gogh's works, and display them in the classroom; if possible, include "The Starry Night."

- Play a recording of Don McLean's song "Vincent" to the class.

- Give the class an abbreviated story of van Gogh's life and work.

- Work on the judgment.

- Many middle school students are afraid to commit a judgment to writing. Insist that they write down their opinions.

- If first drafts don't contain clearly stated judgments, return the paper for more work.

- Make sure that students address their papers to van Gogh, as required in the directions.

How to Search the Internet

- Encourage students to check out a number of different search engines before they decide which search system to advocate in their essays.

- Remind students to include some exciting facts they have picked up while conducting the research for their essays.

- Each student essay must include an actual judgment that is made about one particular search method.

- Stress to students the importance of maintaining a clear sense of logic and organization in their writing so that their proposals have the most impact.

My Favorite Web Site

- Tell students that the newspaper for which they are writing can represent either an on-campus or an off-campus club.

- Remind writers to include the complete, accurate URL in their essays.

- Students need to remember to explain in detail why the web site being described is the favorite.

- Encourage your writers to avoid effusiveness in their praise of web sites. They should elaborate on a few good qualities, and substantiate them. Unsubstantiated statements detract from the overall effectiveness of any essay.

Name _____

Date _____

Five-Paragraph Essay:
Evaluative Writing

Directions: The essential element in evaluative writing is the judgment. Write your judgment clearly in the judgment box. Then proceed to note your reasons in the triangles until you reach the logical conclusion.

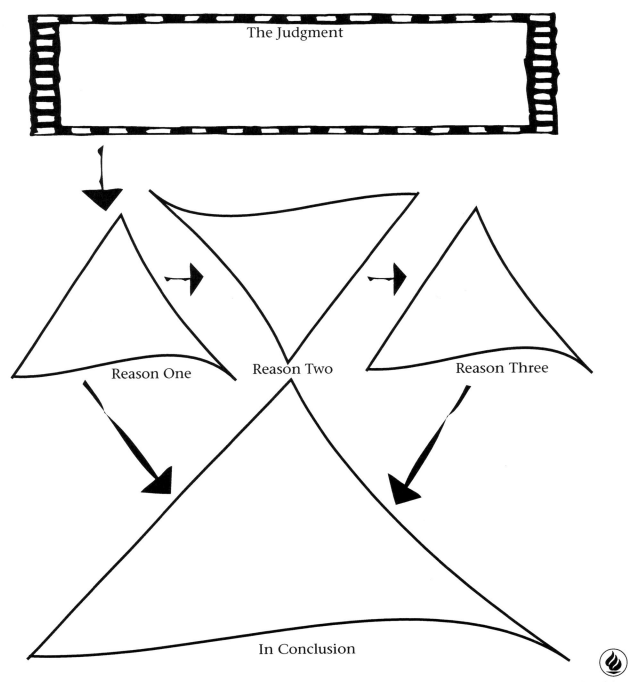

The Judgment

Reason One   Reason Two   Reason Three

In Conclusion

REVISION GUIDE AND GRADING RUBRIC

Name _____

Date _____

Evaluative Writing

Title:	My Auto _____
	The Starry Night _____
	How to Search the Internet _____
	My Favorite Web Site _____

Revision Guide	Y/N
You base your reasoning on facts that support your opinion. Some of these reasons are general, and some are very specific. You show awareness of your readers.	
Suggestions: _____ _____ _____	
You engage your reader. You move through the paper with logic and coherence. You provide a closing that pulls your article together.	
Suggestions: _____ _____ _____	

Final Draft Checklist

Check the essay's needs:

Spelling check _____

Grammar check _____

Verb usage _____

Paragraphs _____

Organization _____

Judgment offered _____

Good facts used _____

Grading Rubric

1 = minimal   5 = exceptional

1. The judgment you make about the subject is clear. The tone is consistent with the judgment. Your feelings about this subject are expressed both emotionally and logically.

    1   2   3   4   5

2. You describe the subject well. You use comparison and contrast to elaborate your description. You use good "showing" techniques.

    1   2   3   4   5

3. Your feelings and opinion are expressed forcefully. You use good organization in your writing. You also show understanding about the objections to your subject.

    1   2   3   4   5

4. You have a strong introduction and conclusion. Your writing contains at least five paragraphs. You use good spelling and grammar. The neatness of the paper shows great care.

    1   2   3   4   5

First Draft Grade	**FINAL GRADE**

8 Kinds of Writing

Chapter 4
Evaluative Writing

Simply put, writing in this style asks you to form an opinion, state it clearly, and explain why you have that opinion. Unfortunately, it doesn't always seem that easy when you sit down to write. But this is one of the most useful types of writing to learn. We see it in book reviews and movie reviews. Any kind of review is essentially a piece of evaluative writing. This type of writing calls for the critical thinking skills of analysis, synthesis, and evaluation.

In evaluative writing, you start off by forming an opinion and stating it for the reader. You must then persuade the reader that your opinion is valid. To do this, you can use comparisons and contrasts, examples, anecdotes, and descriptions, as well as other techniques. Your argument must be supported by clearly developed proofs.

Organization is valuable here and shouldn't be overlooked. Some students find that they are able to make the original judgment but have trouble backing it up with arguments. Try to organize your thoughts on the subject, perhaps by using an outline or clusters of ideas. You should then find it easier to develop your arguments and to lead them to a natural conclusion.

Finally, choose a tone that is appropriate to your subject. Set the tone in the opening paragraph. Then use it consistently throughout the essay to produce a successful piece of evaluative writing.

Graphic Organizer

The prewriting organizer for evaluative writing starts with the central issue of your essay: the judgment. This can be hard to formulate and state clearly. After you have stated your judgment, the organizer guides you through the different reasons that led you to this opinion. All three of the reasons you provide should support the conclusion of your essay.

Name _____

Date _____

Chapter 4:
Evaluative Writing

My Auto

Writing Situation

We all dream of owning certain cars. Each year when new cars are unveiled, people flock to see them. The new styles can be seen in car showrooms, at auto shows, in auto magazines. It's an American tradition to look at them and think of the kind of car you'd like. Many teenagers dream about owning their first car.

Directions for Writing

Write an article for your school newspaper about the car you would like to have when you are eligible to drive. You must tell your readers why you think this is the best car to own. Describe its assets. Discuss its deficits. Make sure you give vivid visual descriptions, so that your readers are able to "see" what you are talking about. You'll want to include a good introduction, and have a conclusion that pulls the whole thing together.

Prompt Notes

- Make sure you go beyond the looks of the car.
- Consider all the different aspects of the automobile.
- Get a car magazine and read about an automotive test drive.
- Shape your essay so that it follows the newspaper article format.

Chapter 4:
Evaluative Writing

The Starry Night

Writing Situation

Vincent van Gogh wanted to sell his paintings, but during his life, he sold only one of them. He was tortured by the fact that people didn't like or appreciate his work. He painted "The Starry Night" hoping that it would be received as a masterpiece. You are an art dealer during van Gogh's lifetime. He has sent you several pieces of his work to evaluate.

Directions for Writing

Write an evaluation of one of the paintings van Gogh has sent you. You must give your opinion of the painting you select. You should give van Gogh the reasons for your opinion. Use the painting as evidence of your evaluation. Find an interesting beginning. Show that you are aware of van Gogh's feelings. Your conclusion should pull the whole essay together.

Prompt Notes

- Look at reproductions of van Gogh's work.
- Learn something about van Gogh's life and work.
- Work on forming an opinion.
- It can be hard to commit yourself to an opinion in writing. A written opinion is essential to this piece of writing.
- Make sure that you address your paper to van Gogh, as required in the directions.

Name _____

Date _____

Chapter 4:
Evaluative Writing

How to Search the Internet

Writing Situation

Your teacher has given you a research assignment and you have decided to do the research on the Internet. You have attended a class or have had some experience with the Internet. Now it is time to explain how you would use the Internet to find any information you need.

Directions for Writing

Write an essay for your Social Studies teacher. In it, describe the best method you know to find information on the Internet. Your teacher will want you to explain why the search engine or method you chose is the best. Your teacher will also want to know the results of the search and how you used the information in a report. You must write at least five paragraphs and use either bullets or numbers to indicate steps in the process. Use your best grammar and spelling and neatest writing.

Prompt Notes

- Maintaining logic is important.
- Check out different search engines before you decide on the best approach.
- In your writing, include some exciting things you have learned while preparing for this essay.
- Make a judgment about your method.

Chapter 4:
Evaluative Writing

My Favorite Web Site

Writing Situation

"I have the 'tightest' place for you to visit. It's **HaveaGoodDay.com**." How often have you heard somebody talking like that about an Internet site? Today the World Wide Web has opened up vistas that no other generation has had available. We can find almost any kind of information for any kind of interest. Often, the hardest part of surfing the Web is narrowing down a few favorites in your chosen subject.

Directions for Writing

Write an article for a club's newsletter telling of a web site that club members would like to visit. Include all the details that would make this a good site for members of your club to visit. Explain what readers will find there and why they might want to visit the site. Use your best grammar and spelling; make sure that you write at least five paragraphs, making the first one an introduction and the last one a conclusion.

Prompt Notes

- The club newspaper can either be an on-campus or off-campus club.
- Make sure that you write the complete URL in your essay.
- Explain clearly why this is your favorite web site.
- Try to limit your praise to a few good elaborated qualities. Unsubstantiated statements make an essay less effective.

Chapter 5

Observational Writing

Chapter 5:
Observational Writing

In observational writing, writers must be able to relate what they have seen. News reporters are trained to be good observers and usually write about the events they see in an observational manner. The techniques a writer develops in observational writing can be applied to all the other writing styles covered here, as they all depend on good reporting of observations. The writer can use any strategy to achieve this goal. The format can be an essay, poetry, journal entries, or letters. Depending on what the prompt calls for, and what the writer means to do with the prompt, any of these can be appropriate.

The first challenge in this type of writing is deciding on the writer's stance. In observational writing, the writer is not part of the action or scene and cannot describe it in the first person, as if it directly affects or relates to the writer. Middle school students find this distancing hard, because their social growth dictates an egocentric world. To solve this problem, give students a simple rule: No *I*'s.

Another distinguishing feature of this type of writing is the writer's view. To write successfully in this style, the writer must have a zoom lens for a pen. As a photographer can use a zoom lens to take a picture study of a scene, the writer can use the pen on three levels. Wide angles are needed to give the reader the whole picture. A medium-angle shot is needed to focus on the writer's major points. Narrow, telephoto shots are needed to get into the soul of the subject.

For example, in writing about a tree, the student might first put the tree in the forest that generated it. The second part of this writing might focus on the symmetry of the tree as a whole. The third part would get into the bark and its inhabitants, each little branch, and the individual leaves that make the tree what it is. These three aspects are then put into a context of time and place to complete the picture of the tree.

I've developed one very successful method of teaching the different aspects of observational writing. I attach a video camera with an 8:1 zoom lens to a television in the classroom, usually through the VCR. I focus on an object, either within or outside the classroom. I then manipulate what the students see by using the zoom. At each level, we discuss what can be observed. Since most students are familiar with video techniques from television, this helps them relate their own experience to the requirements of the prompt. This exercise also serves as a prewriting assignment.

Graphic Organizer

This prewriting organizer is designed to get students thinking about sensory details. Successful observational writers use sensory words well; they are aware of the impact sensory words have on mental imagery. In the introduction, students need to establish their stance and then think of the sensory details they need to complete the observation. Lastly, they must think of a concluding statement that will pull the whole scene together for their readers.

Observational Writing
Prompt Notes

I Pigged Out

- Emphasize the different views of the scene:
    close up—
        the food
        eating
    far view—
        where the whole scene takes place
        an overview of the scene

- This is a good prompt for a discussion of time and place.

- Emphasize fun with this prompt.

After the Rain

- For this prompt, work on long and close views of the scene being observed.

- Emphasize the different senses involved in observation.

- Work on details.

- Similes are good to use here.

- Try to get the writer to share some insight in this essay.

Move Over! I Win!

- Being "in the zone" means reaching a high level of achievement in a particular endeavor (a sport, a game, etc.).

- Encourage students to be as descriptive as possible. They should think their writing through to the smallest details.

- Students should use vivid action words in this essay.

- As the title of the essay implies, the best feelings for students to convey in this writing are those of triumph.

The Empty Room

- You may need to help students visualize just *how* the room is empty, since the phrase "empty room" can mean many different things (empty of people, empty of furniture, etc.).

- This essay is an exercise in extreme imagination. Students will have fun with this if they can let their imaginations loose.

- Stress to students that an "empty room" may still have many things in it. They need to imagine what those things are and to describe them clearly for their readers.

- Remind students to cover all five senses when describing their room.

Name _____

Date _____

Five-Paragraph Essay:
Observational Writing

Directions: Think about how you would like to introduce what you are observing. In the top graphic, write notes to remind you about it. Then fill each box with notes for your essay. In the last box, figure out how you want to end your essay.

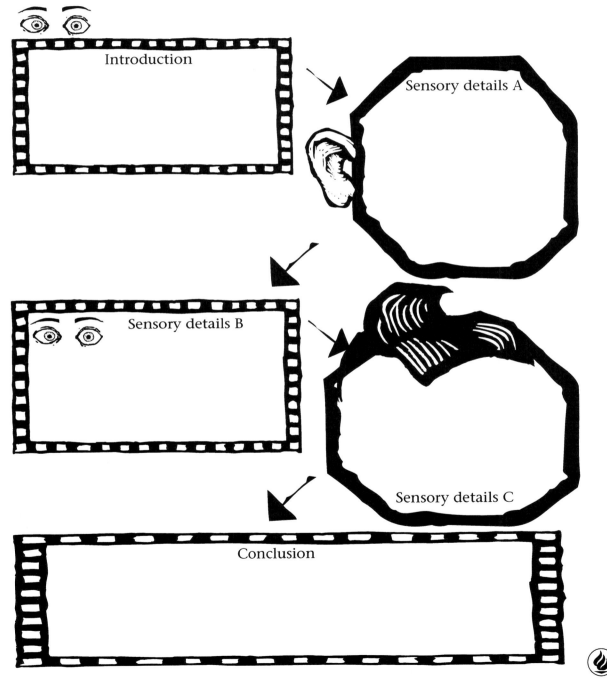

Introduction

Sensory details A

Sensory details B

Sensory details C

Conclusion

Name _____

Date _____

Observational Writing

Title: I Pigged Out _____
After the Rain _____
Move Over! I Win! _____
The Empty Room _____

Revision Guide	Y/N
You start the essay in a way that makes me want to keep reading. Your essay proceeds logically. You have a good conclusion.	
Suggestions: _____ _____ _____	
You are a good observer. You show the scene both close up and far away. You make use of the different senses in your writing.	
Suggestions: _____ _____ _____	

Final Draft Checklist

Check the essay's needs:

Spelling check _____
Grammar check _____
Verb usage _____
Paragraphs _____
Organization _____
Observing _____
Three views _____
Sensory words _____

Grading Rubric

1 = minimal   5 = exceptional

1. Your paper defines and identifies the observed subject. You use correct writing strategies.

    1   2   3   4   5

2. You are a good observer and convey what you observe in a way that is exciting and interesting.

    1   2   3   4   5

3. You have shown your subject from all three angles of writing. Each level is shown in a way that makes clear its relationship to the observer.

    1   2   3   4   5

4. You have a strong introduction and conclusion. Your writing contains at least five paragraphs. You use good spelling and grammar. The neatness of the paper shows great care.

    1   2   3   4   5

First Draft Grade	**FINAL GRADE**

8 Kinds of Writing

STUDENT INFORMATION SHEET

Name _____

Date _____

Chapter 5
Observational Writing

In observational writing, you must be able to relate what you have seen. The techniques you develop for this style of writing will also help you with other writing styles. Most writing depends on good reporting of observations. News reporters are trained to be good observers. They usually use an observational style to write about the events they see.

You can use any strategy to achieve the goal of clear observational writing. The format can be an essay, poetry, journal entries, or letters. Depending on what the prompt calls for, and what you mean to do with the prompt, any of these can be appropriate.

The first challenge in this type of writing is deciding on your stance. Remember that you are observing a scene; you are not part of it. You cannot describe the action in the first person, as if it directly affects you. You may find it hard to describe a scene in this way, as if from a distance. One simple rule can be a help: **no *I's***. If you keep from using the first person, you'll find it far easier to write in a truly observational style.

Another distinguishing feature of this type of writing is the writer's view. To write successfully in this style, you must have a zoom lens for a pen. As a photographer can use a zoom lens to take a picture study of a scene, you can use the pen on three levels. You need wide angles to give the reader the whole picture. You need a medium-angle shot to focus on your major points. You

need narrow, telephoto shots to get into the soul of the subject.

For example, in writing about a tree, you might first put the tree in the forest that generated it. The second part of this writing might focus on the symmetry of the whole tree. The third part would get into the bark and its inhabitants, each little branch, and the individual leaves that make the tree what it is. You then put these three aspects into the context of time and place to complete the picture of the tree.

Graphic Organizer

The prewriting organizer for observational writing will get you thinking about sensory details. Successful observational writers use sensory words well; they are aware of the impact such words have on their readers' mental imagery. Establish your position in the introduction. Then think of the sensory details needed to complete the observation. Finally, think of a concluding statement that will pull the whole scene together.

Name _____

Date _____

Chapter 5:
Observational Writing

I Pigged Out

Writing Situation

Every so often we see a meal that cannot be resisted. It might be in conjunction with a holiday, a special event, or some family occasion. In any case, the food at this event is irresistible. As we start eating, we heap our plates to overflowing. Often this kind of meal is so good that it becomes a cherished memory. The afterglow seems to grow as the memories are relived.

Directions for Writing

Write an essay for your English teacher describing a great meal you have eaten. Your teacher will want to know why this meal was served, who else was there to enjoy it, what happened during the meal. Your teacher will also want to know how the food tasted. You will need to write word pictures showing the food and the actions of the people around you. Last, your teacher will want to know the significance of this meal in your life.

Prompt Notes

- Emphasize the different views of the scene:
  close up—
    the food
    eating
  far view—
    where the whole scene takes place
    an overview of the scene
- Remember to place your scene within a context of time and place.
- Don't be afraid to have fun with this paper.

Chapter 5:
Observational Writing

After the Rain

Writing Situation

One of the best times to be outdoors is right after a rainstorm. It seems that the longer the rain lasts, the better the period after the rain is. The air smells fresh; birds are singing; life seems to renew itself.

Directions for Writing

Write an essay for your English teacher that describes the period of time right after a rainstorm. Your teacher will be looking for details. You will be expected to show the scene from several different views. You should include all the senses that are involved in appreciating the scene after a rainstorm.

Prompt Notes

- For this paper, work on long and close views of the scene being observed.
- Emphasize the different senses involved in observation.
- Work on details.
- Similes are good to use here.
- Try to share some insight in this essay.

Chapter 5:
Observational Writing

Move Over! I Win!

Writing Situation

You and your friends often compare video games. You have just found a game that is so great you want to tell the world about it. You pour out all the details to your friends and get excited all over again. Now you want to write about the game to tell more people about it. You do this at your first opportunity.

Directions for Writing

Write an article for your school newspaper about a time when you were "in the zone" while playing a video or computer game. You will want to convey the excitement of this triumph in your writing. Write about every great move you made during this game. Show all the characters in the game and explain their function. Show how you defeated the villains. Remember to reveal your feelings as you moved through the game. Don't forget to check your grammar and spelling. Write at least five paragraphs.

Prompt Notes

- Being "in the zone" means that things that are normally hard for you become easy.

- This is an opportunity to really be descriptive. Think about the smallest details.

- Think of action words that describe actions.

- The best feelings to convey are those of triumph.

Name _____

Date _____

Chapter 5:
Observational Writing

The Empty Room

Writing Situation

You are a psychic. You can see things that aren't there in empty spaces. Your mission today is to peer into a room that has been vacated and let us all know what it is like inside. Your mission is to make this scene come alive in our minds.

Directions for Writing

Write an essay for your English teacher describing the inside of an empty room. Your teacher will want to know all the details of the room, what you observe. Your teacher will want you to recount this scene with great sensory detail. That is, you should use sight, touch, taste, smell, and hearing in your description. You should also use great detail in your essay.

Prompt Notes

- First, decide how this room is empty. There are all kinds of empty rooms.

- This is an exercise in extreme imagination. You should be able to have fun with this prompt if you use your imagination.

- An empty room has all kinds of things in it. Your job is to imagine them.

- Make sure you cover all the senses.

Chapter 6 | Problem/Solution Writing

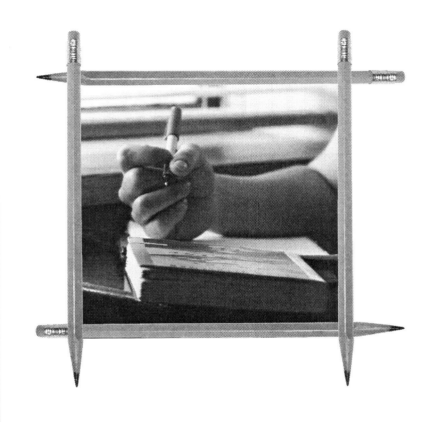

Chapter 6:
Problem/Solution Writing

"Your product is defective. . . . I would like you to . . .". These two statements are the essence of problem/solution writing. In this type of writing, the writer first states a problem, then describes and analyzes it. The next job is to propose solutions for the problem. The writing is not complete until both problem and solution have been presented.

To do this kind of writing, students must gather and examine evidence, and come to a conclusion about the evidence. They must then offer some kind of solution to the problem. Practice at this type of writing improves the critical thinking skills of analysis, synthesis, and evaluation.

The proposed solution should have several facets. First, students must understand that the person being written to also has a point of view. This point of view must be taken into account. Second, students must understand that the solution should be reasonable; they can't propose outlandish solutions. Even if a student uses satire, the solution should fit the satire. Third, students should offer more than one solution. This tends to make the recipient of the letter more amenable to the whole proposal.

I've found several common difficulties in teaching students to write in this fashion. One difficulty is that, as they write, many students forget to put both the problem and the solution in their piece. They may include either the problem or the solution without tying one into the other. As the first draft is completed and turned in, the first thing you should check is whether both these aspects are included. The prompt directions explain that both are needed for successful completion of this assignment.

Another common difficulty is getting students to use factual writing as proof of the problem's existence. Since this type of writing is conducive to the inclusion of students' own opinions, they sometimes load their writing with opinion at the expense of fact. You can point this out to students in the suggestion section of the first draft, or you can mention it in writing conferences with students.

A third common stumbling block is recognizing the recipient's point of view. Students often find it very hard to do this. One way to help them see another person's point of view is to ask them questions, such as, "What do you think my opinion is about this?" or "How do your parents feel about that?"

Graphic Organizer

The prewriting organizer for this type of writing is very simple. It asks students to divide their thoughts into **problem** and **solution**. It then asks them for a conclusion to the problem. Make sure that students put all their thoughts down. They tend to short-change this process.

Problem/Solution Writing
Prompt Notes

No Money

- Students should propose several solutions for the problem given in the prompt.
- Make sure students write for a group.
- Talk about tone when writing to someone in a superior position.
- Try to get students to go beyond the simple solutions of car washes, bake sales, etc.

Oh! The Disapproval

- This is a good prompt to introduce the uses of dialogue in writing.
- Make sure students clearly identify the problem.
- The behavior leading to the disapproval also needs to be identified.
- It is important to include a solution in a letter of this kind; otherwise the writer is only complaining, not really addressing the problem.
- Several solutions should be proposed.
- The solutions must be clear.
- The solutions must help solve the problem.
- One approach to multiple solutions is to give one solution that would suit the writer perfectly, but that the recipient probably would not like, and one that both the writer and the recipient might accept. This way the writer almost always gets an acceptable compromise.

- Students must show that they are aware of the recipient's feelings.

Computers Make Me Scream

- This prompt asks the student to talk about how they solved a problem on the computer.
- Some students have limited experience with computers. For these students, a good subject could be either getting a computer, or how to get a good grade in computer class without a home computer.
- Allow students to use games as a problem.
- Watch for jumps in logic.

Getting Along with a Sibling

- Remind students that bullets or numbers will make their recommended "sibling strategies" more effective to readers.
- Students need to be sure they have addressed their essays to school counselors.
- When describing their siblings, students should show both physical descriptions and specific actions.
- Encourage students to consider and describe their own responsibilities for the problems under discussion.

Five-Paragraph Essay:
Problem/Solution Writing

Problem

   Start with an introductory statement that states the problem completely. In the second graphic, explain more about the problem.

Solution

   State the solution and why it will work in the first graphic. Explain more about the solution and how it would be better for all in the second graphic.

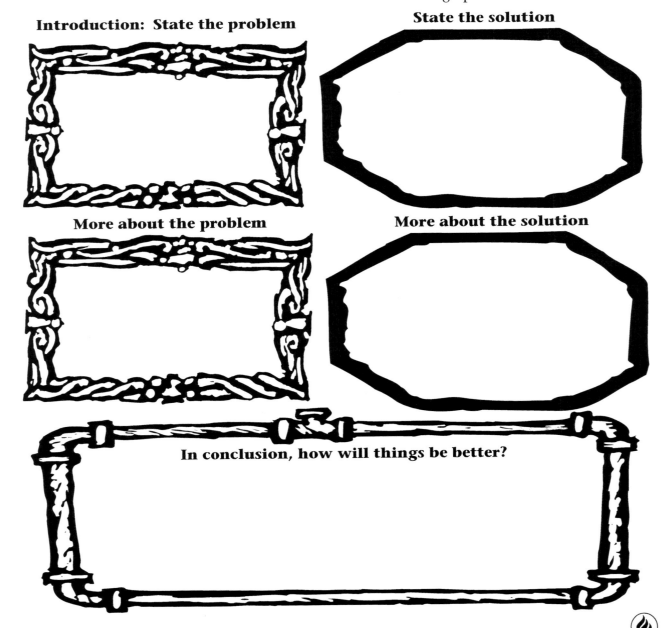

Introduction: State the problem

State the solution

More about the problem

More about the solution

In conclusion, how will things be better?

REVISION GUIDE AND GRADING RUBRIC

Name _____

Date _____

Problem/Solution Writing

Title:
No Money _____
Oh! The Disapproval _____
Computers Make Me Scream _____
Getting Along with a Sibling _____

Revision Guide	Y/N
You start the essay in a way that makes me want to keep reading. Your essay proceeds logically. You have a good conclusion.	

Suggestions:
_____
_____
_____

You included a great amount of specific information about the subject. You are focused and organized.	

Suggestions:
_____
_____
_____

Final Draft Checklist

Check the essay's needs:

Spelling check _____
Grammar check _____
Usage _____
Paragraphs _____
Organization _____
Problem defined _____
Solution defined _____
Bullets/numbers _____

Grading Rubric

1 = minimal   5 = exceptional

1. You identify the problem completely. You also give several good solutions to this problem. You are focused and organized.

   1   2   3   4   5

2. You present both the problem and the solution with logic. You give specific information about your subject.

   1   2   3   4   5

3. You show your enthusiasm by your exciting writing. You display authority while writing this paper.

   1   2   3   4   5

4. You have an introduction and a conclusion. Your writing contains at least five paragraphs. You use good spelling and grammar. The neatness of the paper shows great care.

   1   2   3   4   5

First Draft Grade	**FINAL GRADE**

8 Kinds of Writing

Chapter 6
Problem/Solution Writing

> Your product is defective. . . . I would like you to . . . .

These two statements are the essence of problem/solution writing. This type of writing will help you improve the critical thinking skills of analysis, synthesis, and evaluation. In this type of writing, you first state a problem, then describe it and analyze it. When you have completed this, the next job is to propose solutions to the problem. The writing is not complete until you have presented both problem and solution.

To do this kind of writing, you must gather and examine evidence and come to a conclusion about the evidence. You must then offer some kind of solution to the problem.

The proposed solution should have several facets. First, remember that the person being written to also has a point of view. This point of view must be taken into account. Second, your solution should be reasonable; you can't propose outlandish solutions. Even if you use satire, the solution should fit the satire. Third, you should offer more than one solution. This tends to make the person receiving the letter more likely to agree to the whole proposal.

One common difficulty with this type of writing is including both aspects—the problem and the solution. Some writers give only the problem, or only the solution. Some give both, but don't tie them together. Check for this as you write your first draft.

Another common difficulty is including factual writing as proof of the problem's existence. This type of writing often tempts writers to include their opinions. Don't load your writing with opinion at the expense of fact. Again, watch for this as you work on your first draft.

A third common stumbling block is recognizing the recipient's point of view. This can be very hard to do, especially when your own point of view seems very reasonable. Try asking yourself questions like "What would my teacher think about this?", or "How would my parents feel about that?"

Graphic Organizer

The prewriting organizer for problem/solution writing is quite simple. First, you will be asked to state your problem. Then you will be prompted to state more about the problem. Next, you will be asked to state your solution, followed by more thoughts about your solution. Finally, you will be asked to state your conclusion to the problem. Be sure to include as much detail as possible in each step of the organizer. This will make your essay much more informative and persuasive.

Name _____

Date _____

Chapter 6:
Problem/Solution Writing

No Money

Writing Situation

Because of budget problems (lack of money), your school is going to cut out all extra activities. This includes sports, chorus, etc. Your friends participate in these activities and they are upset about the cutbacks. You have all met to decide what to do about the cuts. Several proposals were made at the meeting. You were voted secretary; it is your job to draft a proposal to the school principal suggesting ways to correct the problem.

Directions for Writing

Write a paper for your group explaining the problem as your fellow students see it. Explain what you think and what the other students think. Propose several solutions. You will be graded on how well you state the problem and how complete your solutions are.

Prompt Notes

- You should propose several solutions for the problem given in the prompt.

- Make sure you write for a group.

- Be careful about tone when writing to someone in a superior position.

- Try to go beyond the simple solutions of car washes, bake sales, and so forth.

Chapter 6:
Problem/Solution Writing

Oh! The Disapproval

Writing Situation

Your parents don't approve of your friends. Your friend Luisa doesn't approve of your friend Marc. Your teacher doesn't approve of the way you behave in class. Your coach doesn't approve of your attitude. We've all heard these tones of disapproval before. Sometimes disapproval makes us feel angry; sometimes we feel rejected; sometimes we feel beaten, or defiant. But whatever happens, we have strong feelings about disapproval.

Directions for Writing

Write a letter to the person who is showing you disapproval. In your letter you should describe the disapproval completely. You will need to discuss its origins and analyze the reason for it. It is important to reveal your feelings. You should propose some solutions to help ease the situation. This should be in good letter form.

Prompt Notes

- Writing about a problem is important because much of our writing as adults concerns solving problems.
- It is important to include a solution in a letter of this kind; otherwise, all you are doing is complaining, not really addressing the problem.
- This is a good time to try using dialogue in your writing.
- Make sure you clearly identify the problem.
- You need to identify the behavior leading to the disapproval.
- You should propose several solutions.
- The solutions must be clear.
- The solutions must help solve the problem.
- One approach to multiple solutions is to give one solution that would suit you perfectly, but that the recipient probably would not like, and one that both you and the recipient might accept. This way you are more likely to get an acceptable compromise.
- You must show that you are aware of the recipient's feelings.

Name _____

Date _____

Chapter 6:
Problem/Solution Writing

Computers Make Me Want to Scream

Writing Situation

Computers are such an important part of today's society. We'll all work with them in the future. It is important that we get to know how to use and appreciate computers. You click, you drag, and work hard at knowing what to do. Still, sometimes, nothing seems to work. You call on friends to help you. They are a great help and you think you understand what to do, but as soon as they leave everything goes haywire again.

Directions for Writing

Write an essay for your computer teacher explaining a problem you've had with a computer, either at school or at home. You will want to fully explain what the problem was and how it stopped you from working on the computer. You'll also want to show the solution in a step-by-step way. You should write the solution in a manner that anybody could follow if they ran into the same problem. Write at least five paragraphs, using your best English and spelling. Your introductory paragraph should be the problem and the concluding paragraph should show the solution.

Prompt Notes

- If you don't have much computer experience yet, you might want to write instead about how you would go about getting a computer for your personal use. Or, you could write about how to get a good grade in computer class at school even if you don't have a computer at home.

- Be sure to keep your essay logical. It is easy to skip steps in your reasoning, which will make your essay much less effective.

Name _____

Date _____

Chapter 6:
Problem/Solution Writing

Getting Along with a Sibling

Writing Situation

"I hate my brother or sister. Everything he/she does bugs me. I sometimes wish that he/she would just go away and leave me alone." How often have you or somebody else said such a thing? As much as we are bothered by our siblings, we know deep down that we depend on them. It's important that we figure out ways to get along with them.

Directions for Writing

Write an article for the school's counselor's newsletter. In it, describe the skills one has to develop to get along with a sibling. Your article should explain about how sibling problems develop. You should develop many different strategies to solve this problem. Discuss the benefits of getting along with your sibling. You should use your neatest writing or best typing. Write at least five paragraphs and use your best spelling and grammar.

Prompt Notes

- Remember to use bullets or numbers to explain something on this paper.

- Make sure the essay is written for the school's counselor's newsletter.

- Things to think about in showing your sibling:
  physical description
  their actions

- Include the part you play in creating this problem.

Chapter 7 | Short Story

Chapter 7: Short Story

For this exercise, students are asked to present a story that is complete in both plot and character. This is no mean task in 45 minutes (the length of the CAP Directed Writing Test). This style is strictly fictional and demands that students develop a story using conflict, setting, action, and plot. Students need to be familiar with these areas before attempting this style of writing.

For this type of writing, students are usually allowed to write in either the first person (*I*) or the third person (*he, she, they*). The choice of person places the story on either a personal or an observational level. Students must realize the importance of consistency of person in writing. It is common for students to start in one person and switch to another person part of the way through the story. Cull these problems out during the first draft.

Setting is developed through the use of details. Students usually need to be pressed to put more details in their writing. Most students find writing the details of a scene difficult. They need to learn how to see the details around them.

The other important factor in the setting is the concept of time. Students often don't see the importance of time in their stories at first, and need to be shown how necessary it is. Let them know about the different kinds of time (seasons of the year, time of day, year in time, etc.) by giving them examples and showing them how time adds to their stories.

Students should also develop character by showing, not telling. Again, you'll need to

do some prewriting work to give students a grounding in these skills. Students should be aware that building a character in a story is more complex than just describing the character's physical features. The individual's actions and reactions, speech, feelings, and thought, all add to the character's development. All these factors combine to create well-developed characters.

Plot and conflict are essential features of a story. You should point out the value of rising action to create tension in writing. Low points need to be included between action points to develop interest and highlight the points of action. The idea of conflict in a story is intertwined with the idea of plot and can take several forms, such as conflict between characters, interplay of character and environment, and internal conflict.

If a student creates a fictional piece that includes setting, character development, plot, and conflict, the result will be an exceptional paper.

Graphic Organizer

In this prewriting organizer, the student is asked to think of the components of a story before integrating them into the story. It's important that students complete the rectangles before working on the star side of the organizer. Students should also keep in mind that setting, characters, plot, conflict, and actions should be spread throughout the whole essay.

Short Story
Prompt Notes

O. Henry's Story

- Have students read "The Cop and the Anthem." Point out the pattern of the first paragraph.

- Explain about life's changes, relating them to the changes middle school students experience.

- Go over the first paragraph again. Show the patterns, and explain how O. Henry uses this pattern to launch his story.

- Show students how the transition is made from the first paragraph to the rest of the story.

- If possible, show part of the film *O. Henry's Full House.*

It's My Family

- This is a good chance for students to use humor in their writing.

- Links between members of the family can be discussed.

- Talk about how our family history and reputation affect our own self-esteem.

- Although this is included as short-story writing, you might also be able to use this prompt as an Autobiographical Incident. With a few modifications, you could also use this for a Firsthand Biography Sketch.

The Trick/The Revenge

- This is written as a story.

- This is a complex assignment and might take more than two drafts to complete properly.

- Tension and conflict are natural subjects for this story.

- Emphasize to students that they need to engage the reader.

- Make sure that students write strong openings for their story.

- Make sure that the opening is appropriate for the story.

- Have students work on pulling the whole story together in the conclusion.

- Tell students to try to get an ending with a twist.

- Students should describe characters well.

- Dialogue can be used to develop characters.

- This is also a good essay to show characters' motivations.

A Day with My Friends

- Tell students that, although their essays should be based on fact, they are welcome to take some poetic license with their writing.

- Students may want to write fairly long stories. This is fine, as long as they don't lose focus. They will need to work even harder on organization if their essays go beyond the standard five paragraphs.

- This is a good prompt for showing the importance of the revision process; revising is an essential part of short story writing.

Five-Paragraph Essay: Short Story

Directions: First, write all you can about the setting, characters, plot, conflict, and actions in the rectangles. Then use the stars to show how each element will be included in each paragraph. Draw an arrow to connect each idea in the boxes with the paragraph in which it fits. Remember to give the introduction and the conclusion some extra thought. The introduction will get people to read your story. The conclusion will complete it.

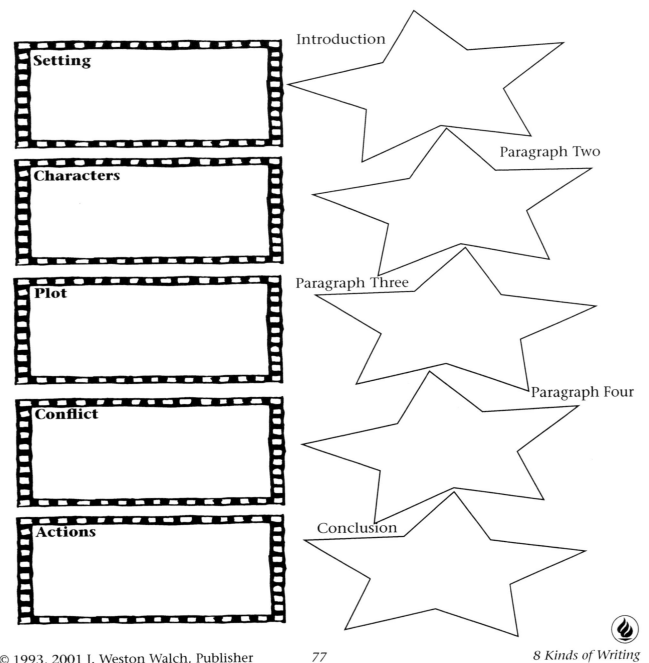

77

8 Kinds of Writing

REVISION GUIDE AND GRADING RUBRIC

Name _____

Date _____

Short Story

Title: O. Henry's Story _____
It's My Family _____
The Trick/The Revenge _____
A Day with My Friends _____

Revision Guide	Y/N	_Grading Rubric_
You have complied with the demands of the prompt in your first paragraph. You have integrated this into your story.		1 = minimal 5 = exceptional 1. Your characters are complex. You show their personality through dialogue and description. You write in a consistent person. **1 2 3 4 5**
Suggestions: _____ _____ _____		
		2. You mix narrative summary and dramatized incidents and descriptions to make your story interesting. Your plot and conflict are well conceived and natural. **1 2 3 4 5**
Your story is well developed, has complex characters, and has a good plot. Your resolution of the conflict is satisfying.		
Suggestions: _____ _____ _____		3. The sensory world and the conflict of the story are made clear through the concrete details, images, and dialogue that you use. **1 2 3 4 5**
Final Draft Checklist		4. You have an introduction and a conclusion. Your writing contains at least five paragraphs. You use good spelling and grammar. The neatness of the paper shows great care. **1 2 3 4 5**
Check the essay's needs: Spelling check _____ Grammar check _____ Verb usage _____ Paragraphs _____ Organization _____ Characters _____ Plot _____ Conflict _____		<table><tr><td>**First Draft Grade**</td><td>**FINAL GRADE**</td></tr></table>

STUDENT
INFORMATION SHEET

Name _____

Date _____

Chapter 7
Short Story

These prompts ask you to present a story that is complete in both plot and character. This is no mean task to accomplish in 45 minutes. Before you try writing in this style, you must be familiar with the fundamentals of writing fiction: **character**, **conflict**, **setting**, **action**, and **plot**.

For this style of writing, you are usually allowed to write in either the **first person (*I*)** or the **third person (*he, she, they*)**. The choice of person places the story on either a personal or an observational level. It is important to use the same person consistently. Some writers start in one person and switch to another person part of the way through the story. Cull these problems out during the first draft.

Setting is developed through the use of details. Be sure to put enough details in your writing. It can be difficult to write the details of a scene. You need to learn how to see the details around you.

The other important factor in the setting is the concept of time. You may not see the importance of time in your stories at first. However, readers need to know when something took place, as well as where. Remember that there are different kinds of time (seasons of the year, time of day, year in time, and so forth). Use them to add depth and interest to your stories.

You should also develop character by showing, not telling. Building a character in a story is more complex than just describing the character's physical features. Include the individual's actions and reactions, speech, feelings, and thought. All these

factors combine to create well-developed characters.

Plot and conflict are essential features of a story. Rising action can create valuable tension in writing. Low points need to be included between action points to develop interest and highlight the points of action. The idea of conflict in a story is intertwined with the idea of plot. It can take several forms, such as conflict between characters, interplay of character and environment, and internal conflict.

If you are able to create a fictional piece that includes setting, character development, plot, and conflict, you will have created an excellent piece of writing.

Graphic Organizer

The prewriting organizer for short story writing asks you to think about all the major parts of your story before you put them together in your writing. It is important that you fill out the rectangles in this activity before you start working on the star side of the organizer. Also, keep in mind that the five key components—setting, characters, plot, conflict, and action—need to be included in all the parts of your story.

Chapter 7:
Short Story

O. Henry's Story

Writing Situation

In "The Cop and the Anthem," O. Henry uses a unique opening for a story about coping with change. In this case, it was a change in the seasons. Many great stories have to do with changes of some kind.

Directions for Writing

Write a short story for a teen magazine. In it, explore the changes facing a student just entering middle school or high school. Part of your grade will be based on how well you imitate O. Henry's opening paragraph. You should have a compelling story that views the change from the teen's point of view. Your characters should be real and complex and revealed in their actions and speech. Somewhere in the story the sensory world of the main character should be revealed. Your story should show preplanning by its appropriate pacing and the satisfying resolution of the conflict and tension you've created.

Prompt Notes

- Prewriting: Read O. Henry's story "The Cop and the Anthem." Notice the pattern of the first paragraph.

- Look at how the transition is made from the first paragraph to the rest of the story.

- Think about how life's changes relate to the changes you experience as a student.

Name _____

Date _____

Chapter 7:
Short Story

It's My Family

Writing Situation

If you've lived in a family for any length of time, you can't help hearing a story or two about some member of the family. The main character of the story might be an uncle, an aunt, or a grandparent. Sometimes the story takes place around a holiday; sometimes the setting is a family outing. These stories might be entertaining, or they might teach a lesson. In any case, these stories help make your family unique.

Directions for Writing

Write a story about your family for the school literary magazine. This story should be one you have heard repeated during family gatherings. It might be amusing, or it might instill family pride. The characters, settings, and events should be well defined and real. These stories often include a moral. This should be repeated. Your readers will want to know why this story is retold in your family.

Prompt Notes

- This is a good chance for you to use humor in your writing.

- Consider how our family history and reputation affect our own self-esteem.

Name _____

Date _____

Chapter 7:
Short Story

The Trick/The Revenge

Writing Situation

Your best friend has played a trick on you. Playing jokes on each other has always been part of your relationship. This particular joke was so well planned, it will be hard to upstage. Now you decide to plan your revenge. This revenge has to be special. You don't want to lose your friend, and you want your revenge to be exciting and funny.

Directions for Writing

Write a story for the school literary magazine about a trick played on you by a friend. Describe your reactions to this trick. Explain how you got even with your friend. You'll want to give this story an interesting plot. Your story must have an intriguing opening. Your readers will want to know everyone's reactions to the trick and to the revenge. Your conclusion should pull the whole thing together.

Prompt Notes

- This is written as a story.
- This is a complex assignment and might take more than two drafts to complete properly.
- Tension and conflict are natural subjects for this piece of writing.
- Pay particular attention to engaging the reader.
- Make sure you write a strong opening for this story.
- Make sure the opening is appropriate for the story.
- You can use dialogue to develop characters.
- This is also a good essay to show characters' motivations.
- Work on pulling the whole story together in the conclusion.
- Try to get an ending with a twist.

Name _____

Date _____

Chapter 7:
Short Story

A Day with My Friends

Writing Situation

It's Saturday. You have nothing to do. You look at the TV schedule, but there's nothing worth watching. You think and think. Finally you grab the phone and start calling your friends. One by one your friends agree to meet you and hang out all day. You are now excited about this day. You quickly dress and get going.

Directions for Writing

Write a story for your English teacher describing a day spent with friends. This story should tell in detail all the events of the day. It should have a plot and conflict. Use some dialogue to present your friends. Your teacher will want you to write in your best showing style. Each of your friends should be vividly described, both physically and psychologically. You also need to explain how these friends' actions fit into your life. You should write at least five paragraphs and use your best English, spelling, and grammar.

Prompt Notes

- While this story can be based on fact, you can take poetic license.

- You may want to write a long story.

- Make sure you don't get lost in this prompt and lose focus.

- Work on organization.

Chapter 8

Speculation About Causes or Effects

Chapter 8:
Speculation About Causes or Effects

Most science fiction stories are based on the question "What if . . . ?" We write in this fashion when we want to propose differences in actual current or past situations. This type of writing generally calls for using higher-level thinking skills.

As always, the opening of the prompt is very important. In the past, I've worked hard at getting students to write unique openings. You might also want to read the beginning of a few classic novels when teaching this type of writing. *A Tale of Two Cities* and *Moby Dick* are two that I've used successfully as models. Students often find it hard to think of original ways to begin these prompts, and use a few tried-and-true openings. I sometimes kill common beginnings in the hope that students will be forced to think of better ones. When students hand in a good prompt with a poor beginning, I give it back. I tell them I can't accept their work without a better introduction, leading to a better essay.

Another secret to good speculative writing is linking the causes or effects to the speculative situation. Students often want to link them only with opinion. This is a good time to give a lesson about the difference between fact and opinion. Of course, students must use their opinions, but they must learn to back their opinions with fact. If you get papers laden with opinion and light on fact, suggest that students include some facts to prove the correctness of their opinions.

In the prompts included here, I ask students to write about changes in their lives. Prompts asking about changes in society—like "What if the South had won the Civil War?"—could also be used here; it's the "What if?" that's important. If the question is "What if?", you are into speculative writing.

Middle school students find this type of writing very demanding. Students of this age tend to be conformists and can find it difficult to think in ways that are different. They can also be rather provincial and unable to think globally. As the teacher, you have to work hard to give students permission to think differently. They need to feel free to express themselves without the fear of being shot down for being different.

These prompts often produce the most interesting papers from students. The prompts should be introduced only when you're sure that most of your students will succeed in this style of writing.

Graphic Organizer

The important characteristic of this writing type is the speculation. In the prewriting organizer, students are asked to focus in on this characteristic. Students need to be sure they have a clear speculation and some idea of where they want to go with it. The three circles in the graphic organizer will help them determine either causes or effects. They need to finish their thoughts with the results of their speculations and the causes and effects in the rectangle at the bottom.

Speculation About Causes or Effects
Prompt Notes

The Big Change

- This is a good prompt to lead you into talking about the changes middle school students go through.

- In prewriting exercises, talk about the changes people go through in their lives.

- Talk about the effects of personal changes.

- Get students to talk about how they see themselves.

Grounded

- Remind students that they need to be very specific, limiting their thoughts to just one grounding. They should not write in general terms.

- Encourage students to fully develop their thoughts about what they might have done differently.

- This essay provides a good opportunity for students to think about and discuss various principles of living. Varying opinions can lead to lively class discussions on this topic.

- Students must clearly delineate the lessons they have learned.

If You Cheat, You're Abased

- This should be written as a letter—a good opportunity to talk about letter forms.

- Get students to see the big picture.

- Work on the tone of the argument.

- Recognition of the friend's point of view is important.

- Encourage students to establish links between the speculations and the effects.

Detention

- Some of your students may never have had a detention. In this case, they will need to talk with classmates who have received a detention in the past.

- Remind students that how they *begin* their writing often determines whether the reader enjoys it or not. They will need to work hard at starting their essays in unique ways.

- Students should describe the cause and the effects in the greatest detail possible.

- Encourage students to write about any changes in the way they think now versus how they thought before the detention was assigned.

Name _____

Date _____

Five-Paragraph Essay:
Speculation About Causes or Effects

Directions: Write a "what if" statement in the speculation box. In the octagons below, note your ideas of what might be different because of your "what if" statement. Each octagon should contain thoughts about only one difference. Write the final result in the box at the bottom.

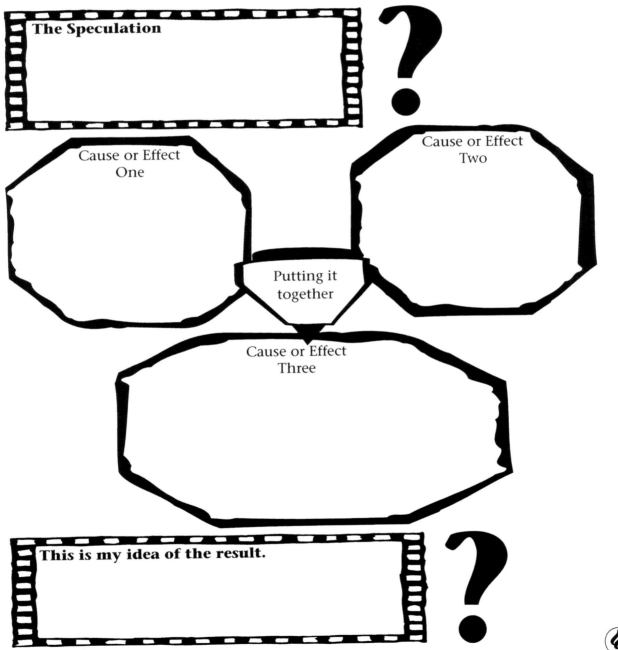

The Speculation

Cause or Effect One

Cause or Effect Two

Putting it together

Cause or Effect Three

This is my idea of the result.

Name _____

Date _____

Speculation About Causes or Effects

Title: The Big Change _____
Grounded _____
If You Cheat, You're Abased _____
Detention _____

Revision Guide	Y/N
You have identified the cause and its effect(s). Your writing proceeds with logic. You have engaged your reader with conviction.	
Suggestions: _____ _____ _____	
You clearly describe the situation. You show awareness of your readers. Your writing is intelligent.	
Suggestions: _____ _____ _____	

Final Draft Checklist

Check the essay's needs:

Spelling check _____
Grammar check _____
Verb usage _____
Paragraphs _____
Organization _____
Speculation _____
Cause _____
Effect _____
Logic _____

Grading Rubric

1 = minimal   5 = exceptional

1. You have engaged your reader with purpose and conviction. You use a variety of methods to prove your point. The speculation is clear and logical.

   1   2   3   4   5

2. You successfully describe the cause or situation. You are aware of your reader's feelings and thoughts and possible objections.

   1   2   3   4   5

3. You link the cause and its effects with purpose and logic. You maintain the proper tone.

   1   2   3   4   5

4. You have a strong introduction and conclusion. Your writing contains at least five paragraphs. You use good spelling and grammar. The neatness of the paper shows great care.

   1   2   3   4   5

First Draft Grade	**FINAL GRADE**

Name _____

Date _____

Chapter 8
Speculation About Causes or Effects

Most science fiction stories are based on the question "What if . . . ?" We write in this fashion when we want to propose differences in actual current or past situations. This type of writing generally calls for using higher-level thinking skills.

As always, the opening of your piece of writing is very important. It can be hard to think of original ways to begin writing. Look at books by other authors to see the different approaches that are possible.

Another secret to good speculative writing is linking the causes or effects to the speculative situation. It can be tempting to link them only with opinion. Think about the difference between fact and opinion. Of course, you must use your opinions, but you must learn to back your opinions with fact. As you write your first draft, make sure you include some facts to prove the correctness of your opinions.

Another challenge in this kind of writing is learning how to think differently. You should feel free to express yourself. Your teacher will not shoot your ideas down for being different; in fact, this type of writing is based on being able to see things differently. Think globally, not just locally, and you'll do well at this type of writing.

Graphic Organizer

The prewriting organizer for this kind of writing focuses on the importance of your speculation. You need to have a clear speculation and some idea of where you are going with it in your writing. The graphic organizer will help you determine either causes or effects and how they relate to your speculation. Finally, you will be asked to summarize the result.

Name _____

Date _____

Chapter 8:
Speculation About Causes or Effects

The Big Change

Writing Situation

You wake up in the morning and you feel different somehow. You rack your brain to pinpoint the difference. Do you look older? Have your legs grown extra long, or extra short? Are you suddenly fat, or thin? Is your hair now straight, or curly? One of these—or some other change—has taken place. People are now looking at you in a different way.

Directions for Writing

Write an essay for your English teacher showing the effects of the change you perceive in yourself. Your teacher will grade this essay on how well you show this change in your writing. You should fully explain the effects of this change on the people around you. Your teacher will want to know your feelings about this change. You will want to give several proofs that this change took place. You'll need to devise a very special beginning for your essay.

Prompt Notes

- Think about the changes people go through in their lives.
- Think about the effects of personal changes.
- Look at how you see yourself.

Name _____

Date _____

Chapter 8:
Speculation About Causes or Effects

Grounded

Writing Situation

You walk in the door one day, and your social life ends. Your mother says, "You are grounded for . . .". You have to serve your sentence without protest, thinking about what you have done.

Directions for Writing

Write an essay for your English teacher telling about a time when you were grounded. Your English teacher will want to know why you were grounded, but more than that, your teacher will want you to focus on the grounding and the cause. Tell and show your feelings, thoughts, attitude, and the effects of the grounding. You should have an exciting introduction and a conclusion that completes your paper. Write at least five paragraphs. Make sure you use your best spelling and your best grammar.

Prompt Notes

- Make sure you limit your writing to just one grounding. Don't write in general terms.

- Make your speculation about what you might have done differently.

- Make sure you delineate the lessons you learned.

- This essay would be a good place to think about principles for living.

Name _____

Date _____

Chapter 8:
Speculation About Causes or Effects

If You Cheat, You're Abased

Writing Situation

You have worked very hard in class. You study every night. You get your homework done and handed in on time. Your grades are often excellent, and you feel good about yourself. But you know that some other students in your class don't take the same approach to studying. They copy their homework. When it comes to tests, they spend their time looking at the people sitting near them for the answers. When they get their results, they never seem as excited as you do. They seem to feel somewhat abased, or demeaned, by their actions.

Directions for Writing

Write a letter to a friend. Tell your friend about someone in your class who cheats. To answer this prompt properly, you will need to show how the cheater has been abased, or demeaned, by cheating. Explain the possible consequences of this behavior. Give a plausible motivation for the cheater's actions. Your grade will also depend on the thoroughness of your discussion of the causes of cheating and its effects on the entire class.

Prompt Notes

- Remember that this should be written as a letter.
- Try to see—and show—the big picture here.
- Work on the tone of the argument.
- Be sure you recognize your friend's point of view.
- Try to establish links between the speculation and the effects.

Chapter 8:
Speculation About Causes or Effects

Detention

Writing Situation

It seems as if it happens in a flash. One moment you're enjoying yourself. The next thing you're being given a detention.

Directions for Writing

Write an essay for your English teacher describing a time when you were given detention. Your teacher will want to know all the details of how this detention was assigned: who else was there to observe the incident, what was the behavior that caused it. Your teacher will also want to know all the effects of the detention. You need to complete at least five paragraphs. The first paragraph should be an introduction and the last a conclusion. Use your best spelling and grammar.

Prompt Notes

- If you have never had detention, ask someone who has had it.

- Work hard at starting this essay in a unique way.

- Remember that the way you begin a piece of writing often determines whether the reader enjoys it.

- Don't forget to give the cause and the effect in the greatest detail you can.

- Don't forget any changes in the way you think as a result of the detention.

Appendix

Correlations Chart: State Standards for English/Language Arts and Writing

Standard	Substandard(s)	Instructional Area	Grades	Appropriate Prompt Type in This Book
Word analysis	Knowledge of word origins and literary context clues	**Reading**	6,7,8	All
Vocabulary development	ID idioms, analogies, metaphors, roots, affixes			All
Literary response and analysis	Literary criticism, analysis of narrative, structure			Possibly all
Writing strategies	Organization	**Writing**	6,7,8	All
	Research and technology			Observational, Speculation about causes or effects, Information report, Evaluative writing
	Evaluation and revision			All
Writing application	Fictional, Autobiographical			Autobiographical incident, Short story
	Response to literature			Short story, Firsthand biographical sketch, Autobiographical incident

(continued)

Teacher Guide Page

Correlations Chart: State Standards for English/Language Arts and Writing (continued)

Standard	Substandard(s)	Instructional Area	Grades	Appropriate Prompt Type in This Book
Writing application *(continued)*	Research reports	Writing	6,7,8	Evaluative writing, Information report, Firsthand biographical sketch
	Persuasive compositions			Speculation about cause or effect, Evaluative writing, Problem/solution writing
	Summaries			All
Sentence structure	Use of modifiers and varied sentences	Conventions	6,7,8	All
Grammar	Parts of speech, Punctuation, Clear references, Editing written work			All
Spelling	Use of correct spelling			All
Punctuation	Use of correct punctuation including use of capitals			All

* Although the California state standards were used to compile this chart, all states have designed standards which are closely aligned with those established in California.

State educational standards for all states can be found on the following web site: http://putwest.boces.org/St/StandardsSED.html.

Name _____

Date _____

Graphic Organizer (Generic):
Five-Paragraph Essay

Directions: Write your ideas for each paragraph of the essay in the ovals. Then use these ideas while you're writing your essay.

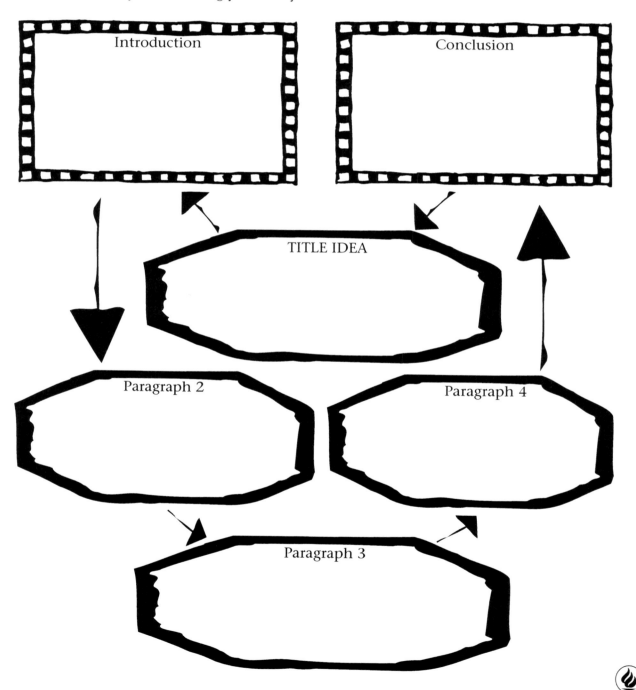

© 1993, 2001 J. Weston Walch, Publisher   *100*   *8 Kinds of Writing*

Name _____

Date _____

Graphic Organizer (Generic): Outline for a Five-Paragraph Essay

Directions: Write the essay's title and type on the first line. Then plan your essay by filling the outline with your ideas. The first blank line is for the topic sentence in each paragraph.

Essay Title and Type _____

   I. Introduction _____

       A)

       B)

       C)

       D)

  II. Paragraph 2 _____

       A)

       B)

       C)

       D)

 III. Paragraph 3 _____

       A)

       B)

       C)

       D)

 IV. Paragraph 4 _____

       A)

       B)

       C)

       D)

   V. Conclusion _____

       A)

       B)

       C)

       D)

 8 Kinds of Writing

Group Read-around Response Sheet

Group:

Prompt:

Class:

Writer _____

Title of Paper _____

Date _____

Reader 1 _____ (Chairperson)
(name)
Write comments below.

Reader 2 _____ (Reporter)
(name)
Write comments below.

Examples of
good writing:

Reader 3 _____ (Secretary)
(name)
Write comments above.

Reader 4 _____ (Compromiser)
(name)
Write comments above.

Group Statement: How well does the writer meet the prompt's requirements?

Explanation:

Common Editing Marks

You can use these editing marks to prepare your own writing for revision. You can also use them for peer editing.

Using a consistent set of symbols makes the revision process easier.

Three /kings walked down the street. ——→ Change capital letter to lower case.

Three kings walked down the street. ——→ Change lower case letter to upper case (caps).

sale
This will be a great ~~deal~~. ——→ Replace one word with another.

The t/he fire ——→ Delete word.

A, B∧ or C ——→ Add a comma.

They∨re over here. ——→ Add an apostrophe.

They're over here⊙ ——→ Add a period.

are
They∧ over here. ——→ Add letters or words.

_sp_
Don't go (untill) I tell you to go. ——→ Correct spelling.

¶ In conclusion, this is what ——→ Start a new paragraph.

_tr_
You should/of these words change the order/——→ Transpose these words.

8 Kinds of Writing

Share Your Bright Ideas with Us!

We want to hear from you! Your valuable comments and suggestions will help us meet your current and future classroom needs.

Your name_____Date_____

School name_____Phone_____

School address_____

Grade level taught_____Subject area(s) taught_____Average class size_____

Where did you purchase this publication?_____

Was your salesperson knowledgeable about this product?   Yes_____   No_____

What monies were used to purchase this product?

____School supplemental budget   ____Federal/state funding   ____Personal

Please "grade" this Walch publication according to the following criteria:

	A	B	C	D	F
Quality of service you received when purchasing	A	B	C	D	F
Ease of use	A	B	C	D	F
Quality of content	A	B	C	D	F
Page layout	A	B	C	D	F
Organization of material	A	B	C	D	F
Suitability for grade level	A	B	C	D	F
Instructional value	A	B	C	D	F

COMMENTS:_____

_____

What specific supplemental materials would help you meet your current—or future—instructional needs?

_____

Have you used other Walch publications? If so, which ones?_____

May we use your comments in upcoming communications?   ____Yes   ____No

Please **FAX** this completed form to **207-772-3105**, or mail it to:

Product Development, J. Weston Walch, Publisher, P.O. Box 658, Portland, ME 04104-0658

We will send you a **FREE GIFT** as our way of thanking you for your feedback. **THANK YOU!**